INVISIBLE TALENT MARKET 1

INVISIBLE TALENT MARKET 2

INVISIBLE TALENT MARKET

Solving the Talent Shortage Without Outsourcing and Visas

Ida Byrd-Hill

Testimonial

Kudos to Ida for writing this diversity & inclusion guide that highlights Blacks as viable candidates to solve the 'digital talent shortage.' As a member of the Invisible Talent Market, I created Blendoor to capture candidate data from existing applicant tracking systems and/or online job boards. Candidate profiles are then 'blendorized' - displayed without name, photo, or dates to mitigate unconscious bias. We are proving a qualified and diverse technical pipeline exists. Our growing database of candidates seeking to match with inclusive companies is 68% Women, 40% Black/Latino/Native, and 26% technical.

Stephanie Lampkin
CEO, Blendoor

Dedication

I dedicate this book to Black Mothers who are fighting daily to ensure their children have a seat at America's Economic Table of prosperity during this digital revolution.

I fought, vehemently, for my children Kevin and Karen Hill to be at that table. Kevin is graduating from Rochester Institute of Technology with a BS in Information Technology. He is completing a co-op assignment as a web developer. I look forward to his continual growth as a member of this Invisible Talent Market.

I thank my mother, Mary Byrd, for fighting to get me into Walker Elementary School for the Gifted. While she did not have a high school diploma or college degree then (She subsequently went back and received both.) She was quite wise to pave the way for me to become one of America's Educated.

© 2017 Upheaval Media, LLC

All rights reserved.

No part of this book may be reproduced in any form or by any electronic or mechanical means including information storage and retrieval systems—except in the case of brief quotations embodied in critical articles or reviews – without permission in writing from the publisher,

Published by

Upheaval Media, LLC
17375 Harper Avenue #241488
Detroit, MI 48224

For Group Book Orders and Speaking Engagements

Phone   313-444-4885
Email   invisible@upliftinc.org

LIBRARY OF CONGRESS CONTROL NUMBER
2017902943

INVISIBLE TALENT MARKET
Solving the Talent Shortage Without Outsourcing and Visas
ISBN (pbk.) 978-098296-10-3-2

1. Business Culture   2. HR   3. Economics History

Table of Contents

Invisible Talent Market

TESTIMONIALS	3
TABLE OF CONTENTS	6
CHANGE IN THE AIR UNDER PRESIDENT TRUMP REGIME	12
BLACKS RESCUED AGRICULTURAL REVOLUTION TALENT SHORTAGE	22
BLACKS RESCUED INDUSTRIAL REVOLUTION TALENT SHORTAGE	30
THE GREAT MIGRATION AND RACE RIOTS	36
BLACK BRAWN VS WHITE BRAINS	44
BLACKS DRIVING MOBILE TECH USAGE	60
UNDERSERVED = ECONOMIC PROFIT	76
REFERENCE	118

Introduction

Invisible Talent Market is a Diversity & Inclusion guide, utilizing economic history of Blacks, to lay the foundation that grooming Blacks with digital business skills is a viable strategy to reduce America's talent shortage, without outsourcing and visas, as Blacks satisfied the talent shortages of the Agricultural and Industrial Revolutions.

This book actually began in 1997 when I was sent by Junior Achievement to teach an Economics class to some 3rd graders at Clark Elementary, the largest Detroit Public School elementary school. As a University of Michigan trained economist and President of The Harvard Group Wealth Management LLC, I deviated from the lesson and taught these students a lesson on the Dow Jones Industrial Average (DJIA) and the Stock Market. The DJIA endured a drop the week after I left. When I returned to the school the following week, the students, full of excitement, explained the stock market drop to me. I thought their teacher gave them an assignment to follow the DJIA. She had not. They followed it on their own.

When those students were promoted to the 4th grade, I discovered they were labelled learning disabled. That should have been private. I continued to teach them economics all year, reaching out to their parents, who lived two subdivisions from my house. On the surface, they lived in the 'hood, but had a very cultured middle class lifestyle. Amazingly these students matriculated to a few of the college prep Detroit high schools and then off to college. They became successful as they had the full support of their newly enlightened parents, despite being labelled and tracked for failure. I pondered this hypothesis - *What if we groomed parents with the requisite technology skills utilizing their favorite tech tools to prepare them for the corporate world. Could we solve Corporate America's talent shortage across 2 generations simultaneously?*

My story
I spent 5th through 9th grade in a suburban Flint neighborhood attending a fast paced suburban elementary and junior high school. I had Algebra in the 8th grade and Geometry in the 9th grade. High schools introduce Algebra in the 9th grade and Geometry in the 10th grade. My parents divorced. My mother, siblings and I moved to a roach infested housing project where girls routinely birthed babies at age 16. That was not my dream. My dream, at the time, was to become a physician and eventually an astronaut as I loved space technology.

I was told by my high school counselor I was not college material despite the fact I ranked 5th in my graduating class, scored 80th percentile on the ACT in the 10th grade, and qualified for MENSA while in high school. My high school counselor judged my potential based on the color of my skin and my residency in a HUD housing project as the other high ranking students had affluent families and lived in an affluent neighborhood.

Mainstream society sees the phrase "***urban genius***" as an oxymoron, judging students in high poverty areas as failures. Everyone, including my mother, knew I was an "urban genius." I was lucky to have her fight for my success bridging the gap with teachers, like Ted Lau, my chemistry and computer programming teacher. Ted Lau was a MENSA member, who dragged me from MENSA meeting to MENSA meeting as my "IQ" he states was "astronomical."

I went on to receive 11 college acceptances. I matriculated and graduated from the University of Michigan – Ann Arbor with a Bachelor's degree in Economics in 1989 and a MBA from Jack Welch Management Institute. I walked into a school in 1997 and pondered, "How many urban geniuses were overlooked because they do not look the way Corporate America or mainstream desires?" While I pondered that hypothesis, I built my career to assist people improve their lives financially. Here is my career history.

ADMINISTRATION/ HUMAN RESOURCES/ TECHNOLOGY

- Managed Employee Relations function for 5 companies including Diversity & Inclusion
- Established contract high school culture, curriculum, professional development and partners
- Created Compensation Administration Program for 2 companies
- Provided customer service and technical support for technology companies: AT&T, Sirius XM
- Participated in computerization of 2 departments and 3 companies
- Managed company computer network

BUSINESS DEVELOPMENT/ SALES/ADVOCACY

- Advocated for the passage of 2 bills that were signed into law January 2010
- Managing marketing, public relations and fundraising for contract school and 3 businesses
- Generated 2200 individual clients and 10 corporate clients for wealth management firm
- Developed client base for executive search firm.

FINANCE/ DATA

- Compile Data reports for public dissemination of event constituents habits and behaviors
- Create Data Mining activities, events, surveys to collect market and business information
- Managed 353 million in assets annually for private business owners and high net worth persons
- Analyzed for small business owners potential opportunities and provided solutions for growth
- Guided mortgage loan applications through the FHA, VA, FREDDIE MAC, FANNIE MAE underwriting
- Closed $1,000,000 of loans monthly with average loan of $50,000

- Decreased the percentage of accounts outstanding 90 plus days from 32% to 6.5%.
- Negotiated a solution with 3 major commercial clients resulting in the collection of $1,980,000.
- Prepared 941 Federal, State and Local Tax returns.
- Participated in Workmen's Compensation Audits
- Prepared weekly payroll

RECRUITING
- Executive Search Consultant Placed 72 corporate executives in technical law positions
- Recruited participants for 3 skilled trades and apprenticeship programs
- Recruited all employee types – exempt corporate, non- exempt corporate, nonprofit and unionized
- Recruited 600 students for 67 slots that expanded to 130 slots at contract high school
- Negotiated salary contracts and fee agreements

TRAINING
- Created **SMART MONEY- Financial Fitness Course** for UAW/ Chrysler.
- Trained 1000 hourly Chrysler employees
- Developed new employee orientation, training program, manual and handbook for employees

I knew my son at 3 desired to become a video game designer as he absolutely loved video games and cartooning. Little did I know I would need to fight for his place as an 'urban genius.' My Son decided in the 4th grade he was going to be the "Black Bill Gates."

His Teacher laughed in his face. She then shared this "joke" with fellow teachers who laughed as well.

My son is a dreamer. His teachers labelled his daydreaming as Attention Deficit Disorder suggesting his move into Special Education. I decided the curriculum that was taught was boring and too theoretical.

In 2004, I left my financial advisory practice to first usher my son into his dream of becoming the "Black Bill Gates." Secondly, I began to assist other families discover their urban geniuses by creating new training vehicles – camps, scavenger hunts, games and community events that utilized hands-on application of curriculum for both parents and students.

I prepared my son ----

- **Intellectually** to matriculate to RIT (Rochester Institute of Technology) to secure a $250,000 tech college education

- **Culturally** with sailing and archery lessons as a member of the Detroit Yacht Club and esoteric vacations all over world;

- **Socially** with a strong work ethic having worked in her Businesses since the age of 8.

Her son is in his final year of securing a BS in Information Tech with an impeccable resume. Despite his preparation to successfully complete coding challenges to secure the interview, he continually faces the cool reception of recruiters in face-to-face interviews when they discover he is a Black man. His classmates secured plum assignments in Silicon Valley and he received a mountain of rejections.

"I coached my son through the lack of tech diversity and unconscious bias to receive his first highly paid substantive internship as a web developer. However, as a mother, I cannot erase the pain of seeing recruiters judge my son" by the color of his skin and not the content of his character."

This book is a compilation of my 12 years of empirical research as a parent, community leader, business leader and urban economist.

Chapter 1

Change In The Air Under President Trump Regime

Feeling panicked that President Trump's immigration and trade policies may reduce your corporate profits? You are not alone.

On the campaign trail, Presidential Candidate Donald Trump vowed **'I am going to be the greatest jobs president that God ever created'**. He painted globalization as a zero-sum game that has enriched low-wage countries while leaving the United States littered with abandoned factories and underemployed workers. He has threatened to tax companies that offshore U.S. jobs, limit immigration and restrict free trade in an effort to return manufacturing jobs to America.

America's middle class was built on manual mass production manufacturing jobs as these high wage jobs required low or no skills. Many employees secured these jobs without a high school diploma as these jobs required more Brawn and muscle, but paid wages similar to engineers with a Bachelor's degree.

Consequently, cities, like Detroit, had few individuals secure post-secondary credentials as they were not needed to earn high wages. As employees matured, their wages climbed even higher. In the 1990s, companies, seeking to increase their profits decided to reduce their largest expense – WAGES & BENEFITS, began to outsource 6 million manufacturing jobs to low wage countries, like China and Mexico. This outsourcing continued until wage rates in these countries began to increase. Looking to keep labor cost low and improve efficiency, manufacturing companies began implementing automation.

Everything from welding, body painting, riveting, inventory, and logistics is automated. Companies no longer need people with muscle and Brawn. They need people with Brains to facilitate automation and to operate the robotics driving automation. Manufacturing jobs have already returned to America, except highly skilled tech workers were tasked with automating the manual jobs that returned. Corporate America has been complaining for 20 years they cannot find highly skilled tech workers with post-secondary credentials, so they began to immigrate highly skilled foreign workers.

These are the jobs that are in high demand.

- Computer programmers
- Data Analysts
- Business Process Analysts
- Skilled trades to install process controls in manufacturing and buildings
- Skilled trades to operate Robots
- Master technicians
- Prototype designers
- Mobile app developers
- Video game developers

CareerBuilder reports these middle skilled job categories have the highest demand in 2017:

Category	% Demand	Sample Job Title
IT	12	Data Scientist
Skilled Trades	8	HVAC Technician
Healthcare	8	Physical Therapist
Business/Financial Operations	8	Business Process Analyst
Sales	6	Business Development

These occupations paying an average of $20 or more per hour, have grown faster than the overall labor market from 2012 to 2016, and have a critical mass of jobs. These jobs require post-secondary training. These jobs are fairly newly, developed to match the 21st century business strategy driven by these 5 disruptive technologies.

Computer Software

$400 billion revenue in 2016

Robots

$151 billion revenue in 2020

Video Gaming

$25.3 billion revenue in 2015

3D Design & Printing

$5.1 billion revenue in 2016

Drones

$127 billion by 2022

Young people and their parents are complaining *"there are no good jobs, anymore."* What they really mean - there are no lower skilled factory jobs that pay wages

INVISIBLE TALENT MARKET

equivalent to an engineer's salary they can secure straight out of high school. They are correct! Today's high wage careers require postsecondary training in iSTEAM *(invention, Science, Technology, Engineering, Artistic Design and Mathematics)*.

Automation Is Here To Stay

MIT Technology Review highlighted an Oxford study that shows 45% of jobs in transportation/logistics, production labor, administrative support, services, sales and construction will be automated by 2033, a mere 16 years from now. Every human being now must have at least a working knowledge of computer software and usage of the internet in order to secure and retain a job.

In a 2011 essay in the Wall Street Journal, software pioneer and venture capitalist Marc Andreessen famously wrote that "software is eating the world." Computer software has been the most disruptive industry impacting every industry. In 1990, there were 778,000 people employed in software jobs. By 2014, there were 3.65

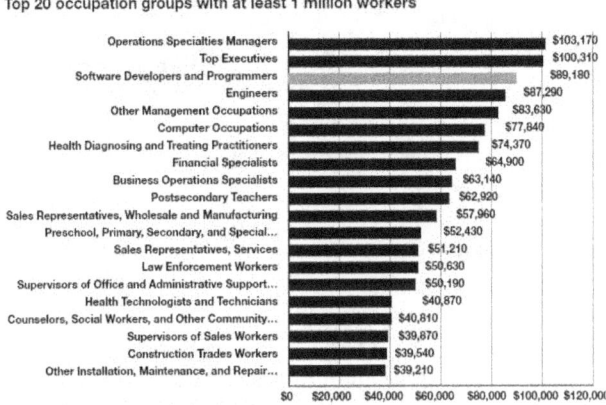

Figure 8. Median Annual Income by Occupation, 2013:
Top 20 occupation groups with at least 1 million workers

Source: Bureau of Labor Statistics, Current Employment Statistics.

million employed in software jobs. The Bureau of Labor Statistics reports that five industries created more than 300,000 new jobs each from 2008 to 2014 – software, restaurants, individual/family services, home health care services and retail. The average salary for the software industry is $86,457 compared to home health care services at $28,278, individual/family services at $23,394 retail at $22,502 and restaurant $15,888. Marc Andreessen was correct as the software industry has improved the productivity, efficiency and profitability of every industry. Its employees have been rewarded with increased wages accordingly.

To satisfy the millions of low-skilled workers who voted for him, Presidential Trump vowed to return manufacturing jobs to America. Manufacturing will **never** return to purely manual jobs, employing low or nor skilled workers. Manufacturers have invested billions in high-tech robots and software to improve the efficiency of their operations and hence, profitability.

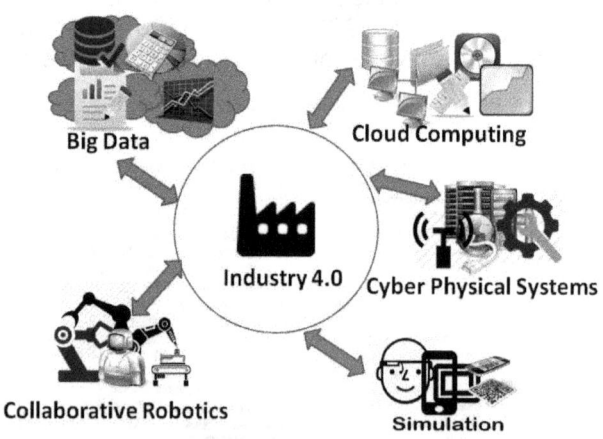

McKinsey & Co. states, Manufacturing's next act is Industry 4.0 where interconnected digital tech integrates the physical and virtual worlds. Computer software is connecting physical robots to the internet to create new products anywhere in the world. Product design and development will take place in simulated laboratories and utilize digital fabrication models. The products themselves take tangible form only after most of the design and engineering problems have been worked out. In the past, industry created lots of physical prototypes until they perfected a product for commercialization. Industry 4.0 will reduce the shipping of parts and products as designs can be created anywhere and sent over the internet to be produced anywhere. Robots have even extended into healthcare to manufacture new organs and body parts from your own stem cells in a factory.

The definition of a robot is a machine capable of carrying out a complex series of actions automatically, especially one programmable by a computer. Robots, now include industrial machinery, appliances, smartphones, 3D printers, and drones. Many of these products are developed overseas in Europe and Asia.

The Real Education Gap
Technology and new products is changing faster and faster. The product development process was once 10-15 years is now 2-5 years. Corporate America is looking for employees who have "**The Four Cs**."

The article, **The Real Education Gap,** Chief Learning Officer Jan 2012, states "The 2010 American Management Association (AMA) Critical Skills Survey showed that overwhelming majorities of executives had begun to emphasize these new set of competencies. The article also states these "**skills are neither intuitive for most people nor taught at school.**"

Critical thinking and problem solving: the ability to make decisions, solve problems and take actions as appropriate.

Effective communication: the ability to synthesize and transmit ideas in written/oral forms.

Collaboration and team building: the ability to work effectively with others from diverse groups with opposing points of view.

Creativity and innovation: the ability to see what's not there and make something happen."

While many of these new jobs are considered middle skill jobs and should be assigned to individuals straight out of high school, companies are requiring some postsecondary training. Few of these digital technologies, in the 5 industries that are disrupting our world, are taught in high school. Very few students are immersed in computer programming, 3D printing, robotics development, video game or simulation development, or drone manufacturing, K-12 schools are not requiring classes for Industry 4.0. Many students could move directly into the work force if they took classes in these 5 disruptive industries. Graduation course requirements look exactly the same across the US, except a few pioneering states, like Virginia, who have instituted 2 high school graduation diplomas –

Advanced for University bound students
Four extra Math and Science classes and a graduation assessment exam

Standard for Career bound students
Passage of a board approved career & technical education credential exam.

While software is eating the world, computer programming is not a required class. It should be. Many students are not exposed to computer programming, nor future technology. Sadly, many high schools require a computer applications class which teaches usage of Microsoft office software. A class of this type should be required in elementary (K-5), not high school.

Computer programming is hands-on critical thinking and problem solving which is grounded in the mastery of mathematics - Algebra, Geometry, and Trigonometry. Many states, like, Michigan did not require these math classes to graduate from high school until 2011. Hence, there is an intense talent shortage as Americans are afraid of advanced mathematics.

America's Struggle with Math Proficiency
American K-12 schools are struggling to teach the basic subjects of math/ science that are the foundation of this fast paced technology. Our global colleagues have far surpassed us.

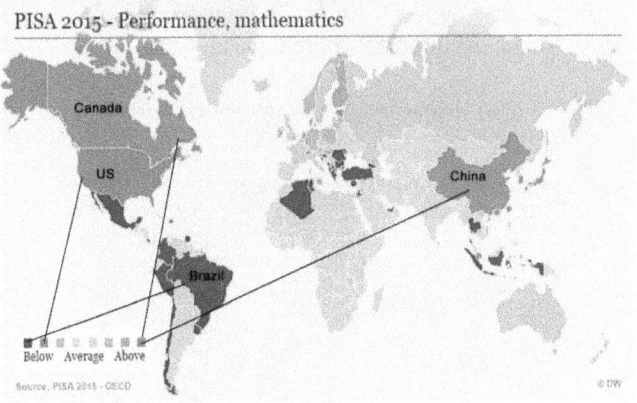

To illustrate this point, America participates in The Programme for International Student Assessment (PISA) a triennial international survey which aims to evaluate education systems worldwide by testing the skills and knowledge of 15-year-old students. Among the 34 Organization for Economic Co-Operation and

Development (OECD) countries, Americans are losing this global competition as we are ranked **26** out of **35** on 2012 PISA Math exam.

In 2015 over half a million students, representing 28 million 15-year-olds in 72 countries and economies, were assessed in science, mathematics, reading, collaborative problem solving and financial literacy. Notice the US is ranked close to third world developing nations in Central, South America, Asia and the Middle East.

High schools are not equipped to teach the synergistic integration of this digital technology. So companies are relying on post-secondary institutions to pick up the slack. Post-secondary institutions are struggling to graduate students prepared for this digital technology revolution as students are unable to master the mathematics and graduate with the credential – certificate, Associate's or Bachelor's. Companies, attempting to ensure they have skilled employees, have increased post-secondary credentials required for middle skilled jobs.

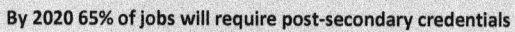

By 2020 65% of jobs will require post-secondary credentials

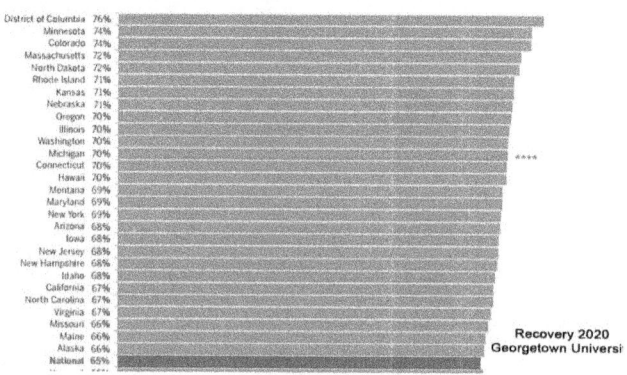

State	%
District of Columbia	76%
Minnesota	74%
Colorado	74%
Massachusetts	72%
North Dakota	72%
Rhode Island	71%
Kansas	71%
Nebraska	71%
Oregon	70%
Illinois	70%
Washington	70%
Michigan	70%
Connecticut	70%
Hawaii	70%
Montana	69%
Maryland	69%
New York	69%
Arizona	68%
Iowa	68%
New Jersey	68%
New Hampshire	68%
Idaho	68%
California	67%
North Carolina	67%
Virginia	67%
Missouri	66%
Maine	66%
Alaska	66%
National	65%

Recovery 2020, Georgetown University

Recovery 2020, a study of the economy by Georgetown University through 2020 shows 65% of jobs, nationally, will require some training beyond high school. Approximately 28 states, like Michigan, have a higher requirement. Despite this automation phenomena that has increased the credentials necessary for employment, Individuals are refusing to secure the training, causing the proverbial 'Talent Shortage.'

Nonetheless, President Trump made a promise to the American people to return "good paying" manufacturing jobs to the US by implementing these policy changes:

1. Build a wall' — and make Mexico pay for it to stop illegal Mexican immigration at the border.
2. Temporarily ban Muslims from entering the US to stop terrorism
3. Withdraw from the Trans-Pacific Partnership
4. Impose tariffs and taxes on imported goods
5. Renegotiate the terms of the North American Free Trade Agreement (NAFTA)
6. Reduce H-1B visas to prevent American IT workers from being replaced by Indian outsourcers.

No one really believed President Trump would carry out these promises as they seemed very farfetched. Well, he implemented #2 and #3 by executive order on January 23, 2017. While Federal court nullified the Muslims Travel ban, everyone knows change is in the air and the talent acquisition strategy of H-1B visas and outsourcing will be slated for a significant reduction, intensifying the talent shortage.

Are you and your company prepared for this TALENT SHORTAGE tsunami?

Chapter 2

Blacks Rescued Agricultural Revolution Talent Shortage

Talent shortages are not a new phenomenon. America has lacked the appropriate skilled labor for every economic revolution it entered during its history. The irony, Blacks have rescued America from every talent shortage. Yet, Blacks are invisible, during this Digital Revolution. Richard Florida, author of Rise of the Creative Class summarizes it best, the creative tech industry "***looks like the United Nations minus Black faces.***" Employers have implied Blacks lack the skills necessary for employment in this revolution, while as consumers are driving this digital revolution. Invisible Talent Market will highlight the progression of American history to show Blacks have, indeed, rescued American Industry time after time and still have the expertise and power to do the same during the Digital Revolution.

Agricultural Revolution

During the Agricultural Revolution from 1619 – 1865 Blacks solved America's talent shortage.

America's southern colonies grew tobacco to export to Britain. Initially, indentured servants, individuals who worked in exchange for their paid passage to America, were hired to plant and harvest tobacco. There were not enough Caucasian indentured servants. The first 20 African indentured servants arrived in Jamestown, VA in 1619 working to receive their freedom. Business owners teetered on the brink of business failure as tobacco stripped the nutrients of the soil and could no longer be planted. Business owners switched to cotton as it was sorely needed by both northern New England and British textile mills. New spinning and weaving machines accelerated cloth manufacturing and ready to wear clothes production causing the demand for cotton to grow astronomically. The problem - cotton needed to be picked manually and there was not enough labor to meet both America's and Britain's demand. Business owners transitioned Africans from indentured servitude to slavery. By 1865, there were 4 million African slaves, albeit against their free will, solved the talent shortage of the Agricultural Revolution.

Skilled Trades, Slavery and Black Patented Inventions

In 1820-1840 while the southern colonies were entrenched in the Agricultural Revolution, the northern New England colonies were expanding industrial machinery and processes to move manufacturing from personal family artisan production to factory production. Textile mills, powered by water and steam, were burgeoning and expanding industry in New England. Machines were lightening the laborious load Americans had bore. Simple items, like Cloth, that was once made at home enough for 1 family, took months to spin and weave by hand, now took only weeks.

As more Blacks escaped to freedom in northern colonies, Northern leaders discovered they were inventing new machinery. Blacks were the skilled trade of that time period. Booker T. Washington presented slavery plantations as the industrial training that left Blacks after the Civil War "in possession of nearly all the common and skilled labor in the South. In most cases if a Southern White man wanted a house built, he consulted a Negro mechanic about the plan and about the actual building of the structure. If he wanted a suit of clothes made he went to a Negro tailor, and for shoes he went to a shoemaker of the same race. In a certain way every slave plantation in the South was an industrial school. On these plantations young colored men and women were constantly being trained not only as farmers but as carpenters, Blacksmiths, wheelwrights, brick masons, engineers, cooks, laundresses, sewing women and housekeepers." In fact, the Land Grant College Act of 1862 was spurred by this dearth of industrial skills of Whites after slavery.

Excerpted from **Chronicles of the Young Inventor – Sam Rolls into Detroit**

Without formal schooling (slaves were prevented from learning to read and write), Blacks mastered the invention process shown to the left. They invented to make their jobs easier. Most slaves were considered property and could not get representation in the legal system, except the patent office allowed both freed and enslaved Blacks to submit patent applications until 1857 when a slave owner challenged the patent submission of a slave. Blacks could not submit an application from 1857-1871. Ironically, these inventions were the force that launched the Civil War. Here is a sampling of some of those industry changing inventions:

Clothes Dry Scouring—Patented March 3, 1821 by Thomas Jennings

This invention combined solutions and cleaning agents that cleaned the clothes without damaging them. Thomas Jennings owned a tailoring company and then a dry cleaner

INVISIBLE TALENT MARKET 24

utilizing his invention. He earned enough profits to buy his wife and children out of slavery.

Corn Planter—Patented October 14, 1834 by Henry Blair.

This invention resembled a wheelbarrow, with a compartment to hold the seed and rakes dragging behind to cover them. It was noted in the Mechanics Magazine in 1836.

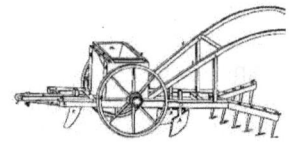

Cotton Planter—Patented August 31, 1836 by Henry Blair.

This invention split the ground with two shovel-like blades that were pulled along by a horse or other draft animal. A wheel-driven cylinder behind the blades deposited seed into the freshly plowed ground. The design helped to promote weed control while distributing seeds quickly and evenly.

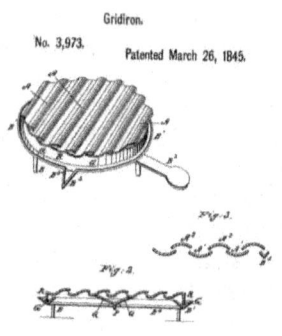

Gridiron—Patented March 26, 1845 by Joseph Hawkins. #3973

This invention is a grill pan with a row of corrugated steel in a standard pan with a heavy handle. Fat drains off of food, the heating process is quicker due to improved ventilation, fewer contact points reduces the surface areas where food can become stuck to the pan.

Multiple Effect Sugar Evaporator —Patented December 10, 1846 by Norbert Rillieux #4,879

The evaporator utilized a vacuum chamber filled with several pans and reduced air to lower the boiling point of sugarcane juice. As the bottom pans heat, they release steam to transfer heat to the

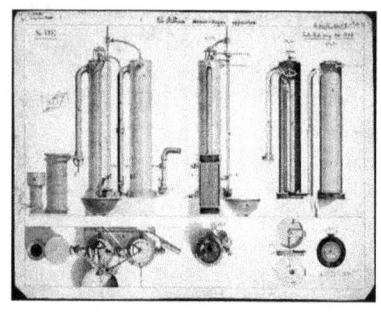

pans above. The heat is more easily controlled because one source is needed, at a lower temperature, for multiple pans of sugarcane juice. This prevents the sugar from being burned and discolored. Since workers no longer transferred the liquid, sugar did not spill and they had a reduced risk for burns.

Norbert Rillieux managed to convince 15 Louisiana sugar factories to use his invention. By 1849, his clients were able to select machines capable of making 6000, 12000, or 18000 pounds of sugar per day.

These inventions improved the efficiency of the Agricultural Revolution. New England leaders needed that technological poweress.

Civil War – Control of Labor to Cure Talent Shortage
"The Civil War was not about morality but rather the control of labor. Industrial companies were growing in the North and needed the strong arms and inventive spirit of slave laborers to fuel it. The industrial companies in the North were earning more money that the Agrarian companies in the South. People were migrating to the North from Europe for these higher paying jobs. But there were not enough people to fill the factories. The North needed the slave labor to fuel industrial growth." The Civil War was an economic war to decide WHO would control the slaves and the future economic direction of America.

"The election of 1860 positioned the nation on the brink of fundamental change." A Republican win would end the South's political dominance of the Union. Southerners had been President of the U.S. for two-thirds of the time since 1789, and none of the northern Presidents had ever won reelection. Up to that point in American history, Southerners had also controlled the speakership of the House, the presidents pro tem of the Senate, and the majority of Supreme Court justices. The Southern states promised they would succeed from the Union if Lincoln won the presidency. In 1860, Abraham Lincoln become the 16th president and then 11 states succeeded to become the Confederate States of America. Lincoln had tried earlier to persuade the Border States to accept gradual emancipation, with compensation to slave owners from the federal government, but they refused. The Civil War begins April 12, 1861.

Emancipation Proclamation - Executive Order to Add Blacks as Union Troops

As the Civil War entered its second summer in 1862, thousands of slaves had fled Southern plantations to North. Many volunteered to become Union troops. The federal government didn't have a clear policy on how to deal with them. The Emancipation Proclamation freed 3 million of 4 million slaves temporarily for 100 days for the purpose of recruiting freed slaves and free Blacks as Union soldiers; from 1863 to the Civil War end May 12, 1865 approximately 180,000 Blacks fought in the Union Army and 10,000 in the Navy. This massive influx of new troops provided the manpower to crush the confederacy to ensure a Union victory. Here is the full text of the Emancipation Proclamation executive order with the clause of serving in the Union Army. **Transcript of Emancipation Proclamation Executive Order (1863)**

By the President of the United States of America: A Proclamation.

Whereas, on the twenty-second day of September, in the year of our Lord one thousand eight hundred and sixty-two, a proclamation was issued by the President of the United States, containing, among other things, the following, to wit:

"That on the first day of January, in the year of our Lord one thousand eight hundred and sixty-three, all persons held as slaves within any State or designated part of a State, the people whereof shall then be in rebellion against the United States, shall be then, thenceforward, and forever free; and the Executive Government of the United States, including the military and naval authority thereof, will recognize and maintain the freedom of such persons, and will do no act or acts to repress such persons, or any of them, in any efforts they may make for their actual freedom.

"That the Executive will, on the first day of January aforesaid, by proclamation, designate the States and parts of States, if any, in which the people thereof, respectively, shall then be in rebellion against the United States; and the fact that any State, or the people thereof, shall on that day be, in good faith, represented in the Congress of the United States by members chosen thereto at elections wherein a majority of the qualified voters of such State shall have participated, shall, in the absence of strong countervailing testimony, be deemed conclusive evidence that such State, and the people thereof, are not then in rebellion against the United States."

Now, therefore I, Abraham Lincoln, President of the United States, by virtue of the power in me vested as Commander-in-Chief, of the Army and Navy of the United States in time of actual armed rebellion against the authority and government of the United States, and as a fit and necessary war measure for suppressing said rebellion, do, on this first day of January, in the year of our Lord one thousand eight hundred and sixty-three, and in accordance with my purpose so to do publicly proclaimed for the full period of one hundred days, from the day first above mentioned, order and designate as the States and parts of States wherein the people thereof respectively, are this day in rebellion against the United States, the following, to wit:

Arkansas, Texas, Louisiana, (except the Parishes of St. Bernard, Plaquemines, Jefferson, St. John, St. Charles, St. James Ascension, Assumption, Terrebonne, Lafourche, St. Mary, St. Martin, and Orleans, including the City of New Orleans) Mississippi, Alabama, Florida, Georgia, South Carolina, North Carolina, and Virginia, (except the forty-eight counties designated as West Virginia, and also the counties of Berkley, Accomac, Northampton, Elizabeth City, York, Princess Ann, and Norfolk, including the cities of Norfolk and Portsmouth[)], and which excepted parts, are for the present, left precisely as if this proclamation were not issued.

And by virtue of the power, and for the purpose aforesaid, I do order and declare that all persons held as slaves within said designated States, and parts of States, are, and henceforward shall be free; and that the Executive government of the United States, including the military and naval authorities thereof, will recognize and maintain the freedom of said persons.

And I hereby enjoin upon the people so declared to be free to abstain from all violence, unless in necessary self-defence; and I recommend to them that, in all cases when allowed, they labor faithfully for reasonable wages.

> And I further declare and make known, that such persons of suitable condition, will be received into the armed service of the United States to garrison forts, positions, stations, and other places, and to man vessels of all sorts in said service.

And upon this act, sincerely believed to be an act of justice, warranted by the Constitution, upon military necessity, I invoke the considerate judgment of mankind, and the gracious favor of Almighty God.

In witness whereof, I have hereunto set my hand and caused the seal of the United States to be affixed.

Done at the City of Washington, this first day of January, in the year of our Lord one thousand eight hundred and sixty three, and of the Independence of the United States of America the eighty-seventh.

By the President: ABRAHAM LINCOLN

WILLIAM H. SEWARD, Secretary of State.

Fearful the Emancipation Proclamation executive order would not survive a challenge in the court of laws, President Lincoln proposed an amendment to the U S Constitution. The 13th amendment passed the legislature January 1865. It was ratified by the states December 5, 1865.

Chapter 3

Blacks Rescued Industrial Revolution Talent Shortage

Reconstruction and the 2nd Industrial Revolution
This time period 1865 – 1914, known as a period of rapid innovation, required Americans to possess a technical skill rather than ownership of one's own farm. The industrial north sought to reduce the cost of production of ready-made goods for Americans and export to other countries.

Innovation is profitable invention. Inventions burst across all industries speeding the expansion of wealth. Transportation, Communication, and Home Good inventions abound linking and building distant, previously isolated communities. From 1865-1900, the patent office issued 500,000 patents for inventions compared to the 50,000 it issued from 1800 to 1869. Blacks participated in this patent explosion as evidenced by the 346 patents issued during this time. Here are a few world changing unknown patents issued.

Improvement to the Corn Husker, Sheller—Patented 1868 by Martha Jones #77,494

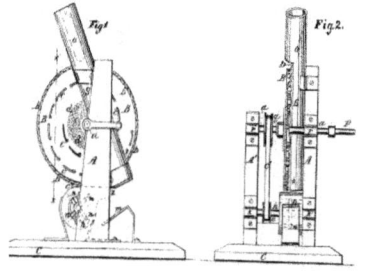

First Black woman to receive a United States patent. This invention could husk, shell, cut up, and separate husks from corn in one operation. This was a significant step forward in the automation of agricultural processes.

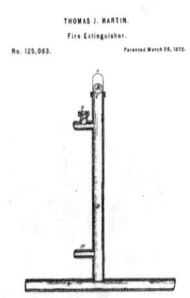

Fire extinguisher—Patented May 26, 1872 by Thomas Martin #125,063

Martin would make an improvement upon an earlier model of the fire extinguisher attached to a reservoir of stored water and used to spray burning fires. Lived in Dowagiac, Michigan

Improvement In Car-Couplings — Patented 1874 by Turner Byrd, Jr., #157,370

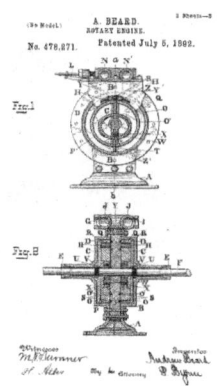

The operating lever with a suitable shoulder, on its outer end, with a catch pivoted to the arm is adapted to engage when the lever is depressed. Many serious accidents may be prevented as the train operator is not obliged to go between cars. Lived in Williamsville, MI.

Improvement in Stove Ranges—Patented 1876 by Thomas Carrington. #180,323

Improved double cooking-range. Heat may be variously applied at the top or bottom of the ovens, and either side of the range, with its oven and furnace, operated and controlled as it heat independent from each chamber.

INVISIBLE TALENT MARKET 31

Lasting Machine—Patented 1883 by Jan E. Matzeliger # 274,207

Molds of customers' feet were made with wood or stone called "lasts" used to size and shape the shoes. He automated the process of joining the body of the shoe and its sole. The machined lasted 700 pairs of shoes a day compared to manual lasting of only 50 per day.

THE SUN.

Typewriter—Patented 1884 by Burridge & Newman #315,386

Mechanical type print machine

Refrigerator—Patented 1891 by John Stanard #455,891

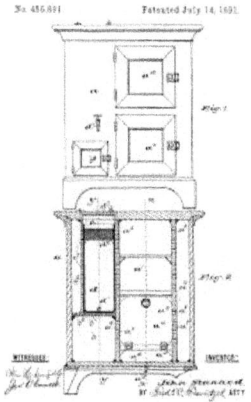

Expanded the Concept of the icebox separating ice from bottles and food. The chamber is adapted for use for bottles over which the drip passes, keeping them perfectly cool. Door can be opened at any time to remove the bottles without necessitating the opening of the ice chamber.

INVISIBLE TALENT MARKET 32

Clothes Drier—Patented 1892 by GT Sampson #476,416

Suspends clothing in close relation to a stove by means of frames so constructed that they can be readily placed in proper position and put aside when not required for use.

Kneading Machine — Patented 1894 by Joseph Lee #524,042

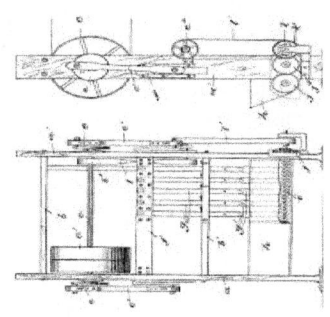

Dough kneading machine to thoroughly mix and knead large quantities of dough and bring it to the desired condition without resorting to the tedious process by hand, saving of time and labor.

Heating Furnace—Patented 1919 by Alice Parker #1,325,905

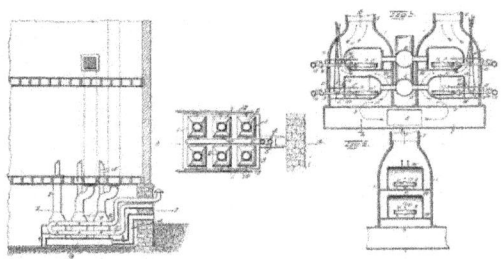

Heating furnace for buildings, in which gas is employed for the fuel. The furnace distributed heat throughout the entire building. It was a central heating system.

INVISIBLE TALENT MARKET 33

Hoisting And Loading Mechanism—Patented 1920 by Mary Reynolds #1,337,667

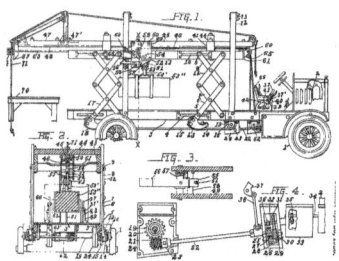

Single operator can lift heavy and bulky articles from an elevated position or from the ground and deposit them on a vehicle, motor truck, wagon and the like.

Automatic Gear Shift —Patented 1932 by Richard Spikes # 1,889,814

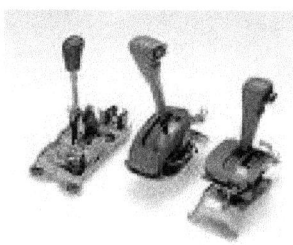

Driver pulls the lever for the speed desired and then depress the automobile clutch pedal. The drive shafts will be automatically connected together at the desired gear ratio with no clashing of gears when shifting. The transmission is silent in operation.

Skilled Trades and Black Codes
Industrial Skilled Trade workers received even higher wages to oversee production. During slavery, Blacks were craftsmen, Blacksmith, engineers and mechanics. Hence, there were many more skilled Black people in 1865 than there were skilled White people. It was natural for Blacks to then occupy the many skilled trade jobs. Due to the higher wages of skilled trade work, there was a good deal of violence as the White worker refused to allow those higher wage jobs to be occupied by more qualified Blacks. Hate strikes, attacks and riots became common place in the North, to intimidate Blacks to abandon skilled trade jobs. Northern business owners immigrated skilled White

Europeans with factory experience. In the South, hate strikes, attacks, beatings and lynchings were utilized to intimidate Blacks, lasting long enough until - Black Codes - special laws that applied only to Black persons, were put into place to legally restrict Blacks' labor and activity. White Southern business owners were "afraid freed slaves would leave their communities and reduce the labor supply." The Black Codes instituted labor contract laws, as well as so-called "anti-enticement" measures designed to punish anyone who offered higher wages to a Black laborer already under contract. Blacks who broke labor contracts were subject to arrest, beating, forced labor, and apprenticeships forcing many minors into unpaid labor for White plantation owners. Here is a sample Black Code restricting employment in the Skilled Trades:

No person of color could become an artisan, mechanic, or shopkeeper unless he obtained a license from the judge of the district court – a license that could cost $100 or more. In 1865, $100 is equivalent to $1,404.49 in 2016) What person having been freed from slavery, with no compensation for their labor, had the equivalent of $1,404.49 to secure a license to work in their skilled trade area?

The chain gang was created during this era virtually returning Blacks to slavery – free forced labor. By the end of this period, Blacks were stripped out of skilled trade work as the Black Codes or Jim Crow Laws lasted for almost 100 years. This period was worse than slavery itself. The lucky ones moved and/or practiced their craft as inventors and entrepreneurs creating products to sell to White plantation owners or factory owners. History illustrates Blacks are inventive people having rescued Corporate America from its talent shortages since 1619, yet corporate and business leaders still see their presence as one of failure.

Chapter 4

The Great Migration and Race Riots

Between 1914 and 1920, roughly 500,000 Black Southerners packed their bags and headed to the North, fundamentally transforming the social, cultural, and political landscape of cities, such as Chicago, New York, Cleveland, Pittsburgh, and Detroit.

Black Southerners faced a host of social, economic, and political challenges that prompted their migration to the North. The majority of Blacks labored as sharecroppers, remaining in perpetual debt, servitude and dire poverty. By the time of World War I, most Blacks had been disfranchised and disillusioned by the concept of democracy, as they were stripped of their skilled trades jobs and forced to remain in poverty under Jim Crow segregation, legitimized by the Plessy v. Ferguson (1896) Supreme Court ruling, W.E. Dubois summed it up well. "He felt his poverty; without a cent, without a home, without land, tools or savings, he had entered into competition with rich landed skilled neighbors. To be a poor man is hard, but to be a poor race in a land of dollars is the very bottom of hardships."

Blacks found hope in the American industrial wartime economy. The war cut off European immigration and reduced the pool of available cheap labor. Unable to meet demand with existing European immigrants and White women alone, northern businesses increasingly looked to Black Southerners to fill the void. The prospect of higher wages and improved working conditions prompted thousands of Black Southerners to abandon their agricultural lives and start anew in major industrial centers. Black men for the first time in significant numbers made entry into the northern manufacturing, packinghouse, and automobile industries.

This hope was short lived. Whites fearful of being displaced by Blacks in jobs and housing began to initiate violence in Black neighborhoods. During the summer of 1919, there were twenty-six race riots in such cities as Chicago, Illinois; Washington, D.C.; Elaine, Arkansas; Charleston, South Carolina; Knoxville and Nashville, Tennessee; Longview, Texas; and Omaha, Nebraska. More than one hundred Blacks were killed and thousands were wounded and left homeless.

Incidentally, race riots almost disappeared during The Great Depression of the 1930s. First to be laid off from their jobs, Blacks suffered from an unemployment rate two to three times that of Whites, but struggled to get public assistance from either the government or soup kitchens for almost a decade as Whites insisted Blacks received assistance if there was anything left. This idea of second class citizenry and the Republican led government's refusal to assist Blacks led Blacks to support the Democratic Party and hence vote to elect Franklin D Roosevelt president.

World War II, Arsenal of Democracy and More Race Riots

The Great Depression ended in 1939 with the outbreak of World War II that spurred an industrial boom and modern race war, centered in Detroit. Automobile factories were transitioned to produce machinery for the war. Carmakers built everything: tanks, airplanes, radar units, field kitchens, amphibious vehicles, jeeps, bombsights, and bullets. Billions and billions of bullets.

Tens of thousands of people were hired and paid exactly the same wage, $5 per hour. Over 500,000 migrant factory workers arrived between June of 1940 and June of 1943 alone. Approximately 50,000 were Blacks. Detroit was a checkerboard of ethnicities, which included Germans, Irish, Italians, Maltese and various Slavs (a very large Polish contingent), all of whom gravitated toward their own sections of the city. Detroit was not prepared to house these people and especially Blacks, leading to a large scale job and housing competition with Whites. Blacks were caught in the cross-hairs of redlining, a practice of bankers and real estate agencies drawing a red line around areas on the local map where they refused to allow Blacks to live in. This left, Black Bottom, an enclave of dilapidated wooden houses that should have been torn down. Blacks, who could not secure Federal Housing Authority (FHA) mortgages, were forced to rent from slum lords at two or three times higher than normal rent. Blacks subleased to boarders to make ends meet, creating terrible overcrowding.

Blacks were given the most dangerous and health hazardous jobs such as iron pouring, furnace tending or spraying paint. The federal government, determined to keep Detroit wartime production rolling by satisfying the needs of Blacks came to the realization that additional Black housing was badly needed. The only Black housing project in the city was the Brewster's and it was full. But where would the new Black housing be accepted? The

INVISIBLE TALENT MARKET 38

site eventually chosen was located on the Eastside at Nevada & Fenelon, right next to a White neighborhood.

Locals were under the impression the new housing project was intended for Whites until it was given the name Sojourner Truth (after a Civil War slave and poet). Whites protested and Washington DC reversed its decision.

Detroit Mayor Edward Jeffries, fully aware of the housing problem and highly combustible atmosphere between the races, reeled off a letter demanding they rescind their decision. The housing project again was set for Black occupancy. The move in date was to be February 27th, 1942, except 1,200 well motivated protestors showed up to moving day, causing Black families to turn back. Later that day two Black tenants ran their car through the picket line, starting off a race riot, Whites turned over cars. Detroit police used tear gas and shotguns to disperse the crowd postponing moving day indefinitely. In tandem with 1,100 Detroit police officers, Mayor Jeffries was granted 1,600 National Guardsmen to secure the route and site. Tenants moved in April 28, 1942.

The world famous Packard Motor Car Company was humming 24 hours/7 days with the vital production of the giant Rolls-Royce aircraft engines and twelve cylinder Packard marine engines. UAW leadership outwardly supported integration of its work force, however, its rank and file refused to work side by side with Blacks. Packard promoted three Blacks to work on the assembly line next to Whites. A plant-wide hate strike of 25,000 Whites walked off the job, bringing war production to a screeching halt. A voice with a Southern accent barked over the loudspeaker, "I'd rather see Hitler and Hirohito win than work next to a Nigger." Black workers were relocated, leaving hostile racism smoldering. Sunday June 20, 1943 was a typical ninety-one degree summer day. Approximately 100,000 Detroiters were on Belle Isle. At 10 pm as thousands of patrons begin to leave the island, a race riot erupted on the Belle Isle Bridge. White sailors from the adjacent naval armory joined in the fight. Riot quickly spread to nearby streets.

The next day, White mobs attempting to invade Black Bottom, the neighborhood where Blacks lived, met with sniper shots from the Black occupied Frazer Hotel. FDR had to divert federal troops from fighting the Nazis to descend on Detroit to quell the 15000 or more White mobsters attempting to destroy Black Bottom. This race riot ended June 22, 1943 with 34 dead - 9 Whites and 25 Blacks, 2 million in damages equivalent to 35 million today, 675 injured and 1895 arrested. There were many race riots in 1943 due to job and housing competition but the Detroit race riot was considered the worse in American history, causing FDR great embarrassment as the American democracy movement worldwide did not apply to American Blacks.

Although discrimination remained widespread during the war, African Americans secured more jobs at better wages in a greater range of occupations than ever before.

Cold Wars and More Race Riots
The Cold War was a battle between ideologies. Communism vs Democracy. The war began in 1951 as a propaganda war. When Korea became embroiled in a civil

war. Russia supported North Korea and America supported South Korea. Again, Blacks were drafted to fight for Democracy despite the fact they did not have democracy in America themselves. Blacks made up to 10% of the general population, but comprised 12.8% of the draft inductees from 1951-1954. The physical War ended in 1954. Almost as soon as it ended, Vietnam entered into a civil conflict that lasted until 1973. Approximately 13.2% of Blacks were drafted into the Vietnam conflict larger than their 11.1% population in general society.

Blacks simmered with anger as they were denied rights at home while simultaneously being drafted to fight the Cold War in supporting democracy broad. Blacks endured police brutality, inferior overcrowded segregated housing, poorly resourced segregated schools and rising unemployment. These harsh conditions prompted race riots.

Race riots grew out of control. There were over 750 race between 1955 and 1973. Here are the 33 major race riots during that time period:

1958: Battle of Hayes Pond (Maxton, NC)
1962: Ole Miss Riot, (Oxford, MS)
1963: Birmingham Riot of 1963, Birmingham, AL
1963: Cambridge riot of 1963 (Cambridge, MD)
1963: Lexington Riot, (Lexington, NC)
1964: Harlem Riot of 1964 (Manhattan, C)
1964: Rochester riot (Rochester, NY)
1964: North Philadelphia race riot (of Philadelphia, PA)
1965: Watts Riots (Los Angeles, CA)
1966: Division Street Riots (Chicago, IL)
1966: Hough Riots (Hough community, Cleveland, OH)
1966: North Omaha, Nebraska (Omaha, NE)
1967: Roxbury riots, (Boston, MA)
1967: Tampa riots, (Tampa, FL)
1967: Texas Southern University Riot (Houston, TX)
1967: Detroit riot (Detroit, MI)

1967: Buffalo riot (Buffalo, NY)
1967: Milwaukee Riot (Milwaukee, WI)
1967: Minneapolis North Side Riots (Minneapolis, MN)
1967: Newark riots (Newark, NJ)
1967: Plainfield riots (Plainfield, NJ)
1967: Cincinnati riots (Cincinnati, OH)

1967 Detroit Riot Image courtesy of Detroit Free Press Public Domain

1968: Orangeburg Massacre (Orangeburg, SC)
1968: ML King, Jr. Riots following the assassination
1968: Baltimore riot of 1968 (Baltimore, MD)
1968: Chicago West Side riots (Chicago, IL)
1968: Louisville riots of 1968 (Louisville, KY)
1968 Washington, D.C. riots (Washington, D.C.)
1968: Wilmington riots (Wilmington, DE)
1968: Glenville shootout and riot (Cleveland, OH)
1969: York Race Riot (York, PA)
1970: May 11 Race Riot (Augusta, GA)
1970: Jackson State killings (NJ)

These race riots forced fundamental changes in American society and business in the Black community. The National Bureau of Economic Research states race riots damaged the Black community economically. There is a perception that property risk is higher in inner city neighborhoods than before the riots, causing insurance premiums to rise. Police and fire protection increased.

Municipal bonds were more difficult to place and taxes for increased. Retail outlets closed. Businesses and employment opportunities relocated to middle and higher neighborhoods. Middle and higher income households moved away. Burned out buildings and blight became an eyesore.

Yes, it appears race riots killed Black communities. However, for Blacks, the race riots provided REAL freedom - freedom to build wealth, buy homes, and attend secondary schools and colleges. Houses are the core of a persons' wealth. Blacks were unable to purchase housing in certain neighborhoods due to racial municipal zoning outlawed in 1917, private racial covenants outlawed in 1948. Race Riots forced the Federal Housing Authority (FHA) to stop the institutional racist underwriting that prevented Blacks from receiving federally insured mortgages with low down payments for homes in their neighborhoods 1934-1968.I bought my first house in Detroit in 1993 with a FHA mortgage. The title work had a racial restrictive covenant clause, "not to sell to Niggers."

Blacks paid taxes to be legally relegated to a world of inferiority executed by local, state and federal governments institutions that excluded them from a normal way of life zapping their political freedom, and economic mobility for well over 350 years. To survive, Blacks cultivated personal and social traits, mores and ethical values different from that of Whites. Nonetheless, Blacks survived and a few thrived in a country that orchestrated their demise at every turn.

But to think current leaders believes as PBS in its The War at Home states, "African-Americans often seem to deviate from acceptable standards of conduct. They become, in the view of Whites, a race prone to violence, illegitimacy, venereal disease, broken homes, a people who threaten property value, make low scores on intelligence tests, and lower standards in public schools."

Chapter 5

Black Brawn Vs White Brains

Rise of the Creative Class states, "*The great transition from the agricultural to the industrial age was of course based upon natural resources and physical labor power and ultimately gave rise to giant factory complexes in places like Detroit and Pittsburgh. The previous shift substituted one set of physical inputs (land and human labor) for another (raw materials and physical labor) while the current one (digital) is based fundamentally on human intelligence, knowledge and creativity.*

Human creativity is the ultimate economic resource. The ability to come up with new ideas and better ways of doing things is ultimately what raises productivity and thus living standards." America has one of the highest standards of living in the world. Individuals immigrate to its shores for the opportunity to earn a higher living. To ensure its continual growth, America's forefathers devised a system to choose leaders – **COLLEGE**.

Thomas Jefferson postulated a plan for public education as early as 1778 that leads to college for the best and brightest. It called for three distinct grades of education: elementary schools for all children; secondary schools further common education for the more capable; college and university for the teaching of the sciences in their highest degree to the best and brightest.

Each ward had a common school on the elementary level (1st -4th) for the teaching of reading, writing, and arithmetic. Each child would attend three years free of charge. Annually, one "**genius**" would be selected from each school every year or two for six more years of advanced study in a secondary school (5th grade through

INVISIBLE TALENT MARKET 44

11th) where they would study Greek, Latin, geography and higher arithmetic.

At the end of the six years, the best ten of the twenty would be sent on to a university for three years and the rest dismissed." The best ten were selected based on admissions essays until 1869 when Harvard and MIT began administering admissions exams with algebra, geometry, geography and Latin questions. The admissions exams were rigorous. Yet, 88% of applicants passed them in 1869. Their secondary schools thoroughly prepared them for successful passage.

The entire purpose of secondary school is to prepare students for matriculation to universities/colleges, careers and their path to leadership economically.

Education has always paid

| No High School Diploma $24,492/yr | High School Diploma $33,904/yr | Associate Degree $40,820/yr | Bachelor's Degree $55,432/yr | Master's Degree $67,600/yr | Doctoral Degree $84,448/yr | Professional Degree $90,720/yr |

2017 Avance based on 2012 median income

Those with higher levels of degrees have always earned more money, especially those with professional degrees, such as JD (Juris Doctorate) or MD (Medical Degree). A person with high school diploma will almost triple their yearly income if they secured a professional degree and will double their income if they secure a master's degree. It pays to delay gratification for 7-10 years to earn a master's or professional degree as they translate into more income per year. These degrees lead to high incomes, low child poverty, low unemployment, and low crime rate and overall positive creative lifestyle. Educated affluent people have more disposable income to spend, hence developers desire to capture that income placing their housing, retail, and restaurants developments in affluent neighborhoods.

These affluent neighborhoods attract corporations looking for highly educated and inventive talent to fuel their research and development of new products and services. New products and services create new jobs spurring more resident migration as people flow to areas with lots of jobs creating an upward economic cycle that keeps the more affluent cities prosperous.

Silicon Valley

Every region in America desires to become a fast-paced economic growth engine, like Silicon Valley, the nickname for the 40 mile radius of southern San Francisco Bay surrounding Santa Clara Valley and the city of San Jose.

Silicon Valley had its origins as a sleepy agricultural area with no industrial or business base worth mentioning, except its most notable asset was a university set up by Leland Stanford, a 19th-century robber baron. Leland Stanford was an entrepreneur of entrepreneurs. He was President of the Occidental and Oriental Steamship Company, (the steamship line to Japan and China), President of the Central Pacific and Southern Pacific railroads. He founded two wineries and an insurance company, Pacific Life. Within weeks of his child's death, the Stanford's decided that, "the children of California shall be our children." They quickly set about to find a lasting way to memorialize their beloved son and settled on creating an university.

Stanford started with much fanfare as a disruptor. First, it would be coeducational, in a time when most were all-male. The Silicon Valley brogrammer culture did not emanate out of Stanford as people believe. Secondly, it was non-denominational, when most universities were associated with a religious organization; and lastly, it focused on teaching practicality. Every one predicted no one would attend Stanford. Its first class, 1891, had 425 men and 130 women students.

In the 1940s, Stanford encouraged its students to research and invent with the steady U.S. Department of Defense spending in. The Navy and NASA has always been the leaders in cutting edge research, 40 years ahead of the general population. In 1969, the Stanford Research Institute operated a node that comprised ARPANET, predecessor to the Internet. The internet was not introduced to the general community until 1995 when Newsweek author Clifford Stoll stated, "The truth is no online database will replace your daily newspaper, no CD-ROM can take the place of a competent teacher and no computer network will change the way government works." How wrong he was. True to their spirit of the Wild, Wild West, Silicon Valley invested their entire future on the internet and software development. They won big! Embodying the spirit of their founder, Stanford leaders, focused on disruptive innovation and entrepreneurship for 130 years, attracting individual risk-takers from around the globe. True disruptive innovation comes from R&D,

multiple failures and relaunches. "Silicon Valley residents wear their failure as a badge of honor. Failure means that somebody else has paid the "tuition" for your learning experience, so the next team doesn't have to impart the same lessons."

Post-Secondary Training on Steroids

Employers believe invention and intellectual property is developed by college educated research and development employees. In today's high tech automated economy, INVENTION can occur in a highly sophisticated R&D lab, on a construction site or manufacturing floor with skilled tradesperson or in the garage of an entrepreneur. In fact, skilled entrepreneurs have quickly changed the face of America and its cities. INVENTION of a product or service is the foundation of every new business enterprise. One great idea can set the economic trajectory of a city into an ever evolving upward cycle.

There are 92 post-secondary institutions in San Francisco Bay and 27 in the City of San Francisco borders alone, not including the various coding academies or Apprenticeship programs. In comparison, there are 79 post-secondary institutions in New York City, 54 in Boston Metro, 45 in Metro Atlanta, 28 in Metro Detroit and 20 in Washington DC.

With a region wide focus on formal and informal learning, Silicon Valley has a large population, approximately 59.3% that have post-secondary credentials - Associates, Bachelors and/or Graduate degrees. Notice the spike of college graduates in San Francisco during the 2008 recession. City and Business leaders leaned on their natural DNA of disruptive innovation created by University directed R&D and empowered their residents to get more degrees to expand this research. Silicon Valley groomed its residents, the past 67 years, to explore, research and invent, growing its tech ecosystem into a prosperous economy that continually expanded during the 2008 recession whereas other regions suffered with layoffs..

SAN FRANCISCO

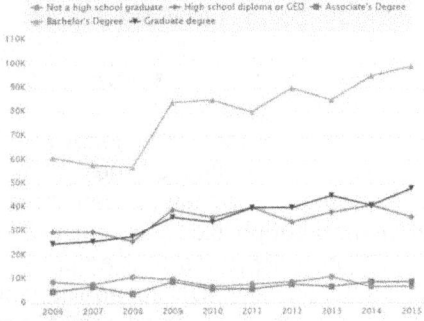

EDUCATIONAL ATTAINMENT OF POPULATION AGES 25 TO 34: ALL (NUMBER)

National KIDS COUNT
KIDS COUNT Data Center, datacenter.kidscount.org
A project of the Annie E. Casey Foundation

Print, television, the internet, fiction shows, advertising and video games show Blacks are savage criminals, who lack personal drive to advance their career and participate in the educational system successfully. Business and city leaders of urban cities with majority Black or Hispanic populations, desired high growth tech ecosystem, looked at their city demographics.

	CITY	% PERSONS UNBANKED[1] No bank account	% NON-CAR OWNERSHIP[2]	AVERAGE CREDIT SCORE[3] based on a high of 850	% CHILD POVERTY[4]	% BACHELORS DEGREE+[4]
1	Miami, FL	20.10%	26.71%	650.64	43.90%	28%
2	Detroit, MI	20.00%	26.20%	589.66	58.60%	15%
3	El Paso, TX	17.40%	8.60%	646.29	27.00%	27%
4	Cleveland, OH	17.00%	24.70%	623.14	54.40%	17%
5	Memphis, TN	16.70%	12.80%	606.72	35.00%	25%
6	Dallas, TX	15.60%	10.10%	632.6	35.00%	32%
7	Houston, TX	15.40%	10.10%	639.07	35.00%	31%
8	Buffalo, NY	14.90%	31.42%	650.96	50.60%	25%
9	Philadelphia, PA	14.30%	32.60%	632.84	38.00%	29%
10	Baltimore, MD	13.90%	31.20%	628.99	35.00%	32%

SOURCES: [1] CFED 2014 [2] US Census Bureau ACS 2014
[3] Wallethub.com based on Transunion Credit Scores [4] Kids Count

INVISIBLE TALENT MARKET

They created economic development programs to lure young White or Asian Males to their cities. They operate out of the same stereotypes as White supremacist Dylann Roof who killed 9 in a South Carolina church in 2016 who ranted, "Negroes have lower IQs, lower impulse control, and higher testosterone levels in generals. These three things alone are a recipe for violent behavior." These ugly racial stereotypes have continued the "Black Brawn vs. White Brains" contention that African Americans are cognitively inferior, but physically superior to Whites and should be kept in professions that emphasize physical rather than mental prowess. Dylann age 22 learned these stereotypes from someone – his parents, his community, his friends. Nonetheless, he spoke what many others believe, including executives in the digital tech industry.

Some city leaders, running from their resident demographics, were subtle in their quest, like Atlanta, bringing the tech ecosystem to every crevice and every population of their region. Others, like Detroit, were blatant in their plan to increase the White male population, blasting their ideas and supposed success across newspaper headlines. Read the headlines

The Detroit News

Detroit's white population up after decades of decline

Louis Aguilar and Christine MacDonald, The Detroit News   11:32 p.m. EDT September 17, 2015

Buy Photo

[Photo: David Coates / The Detroit News]

STORY HIGHLIGHTS

Detroit's white population rose by nearly 8,000 residents last year, the first significant increase since 1950, according to a Detroit News analysis of U.S. Census Bureau data.

The data, made public Wednesday, mark the first time census numbers have validated the perception that whites are returning to a city that is overwhelmingly black and one where the overall population continues to shrink.

TOP VIDEOS

Many Urban cities do have large number of residents who do not have a bank account, which means they have a low credit score as credit is dependent upon having a bank account. With a low credit score the cost of purchasing and insuring a car is prohibitive. Lastly, the lack of job opportunities has caused great child poverty. Business and city leaders, operating out of the assumption Blacks do not desire to move out of poverty, are spending millions of dollars attempting to gentrify the residential, commercial and workforce space to grow an affluent creative tech ecosystem

The growth of the tech ecosystems has revived scientific racism that Whites are genetically more intelligent than Blacks. Even with more White residents, many rust belt cities, have only increased the number of residents with post-secondary credentials incrementally. These cities, like Detroit, still have a low number of residents with Bachelor's degrees and low income.

DETROIT

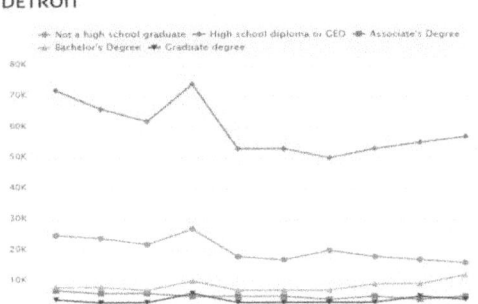

EDUCATIONAL ATTAINMENT OF POPULATION AGES 25 TO 34: ALL (NUMBER)

National KIDS COUNT
KIDS COUNT Data Center, datacenter.kidscount.org
A project of the Annie E. Casey Foundation

Anti-intellectualism
On the surface, it appears Blacks are content with living in poverty and crime. The truth is far from media

perception. Yes there are many Blacks who have embraced anti-intellectualism. Anti-intellectualism is a social stigma of '**acting White**.' Students and families are ridiculed for speaking proper English, for striving for academic excellence and for even attempting to graduate from high school. Even President Obama has noted its existence, in his Keynote Address as senator at the 2004 Democratic National Convention when he stated, *"Go into any inner-city neighborhood, and folks will tell you that government alone can't teach kids to learn. They know that parents have to parent, that children can't achieve unless we raise their expectations and turn off the television sets and eradicate the slander that says a Black youth with a book is acting White."*

Anti-intellectualism is a natural response from being burned out from the war zone trauma of fighting the massive institutional barriers that have prevented Blacks' economic advancement. Lots of blood and tears, from 1619 to 2015, were shed to ensure 24% of the Black population acquired a Bachelor's Degree. Even when Blacks acquire degrees they are often excluded from practicing their specialty as the designated industry refuses to hire them. For decades, Black lawyers were employed as garbage men and postal workers. Many Blacks do not believe 'Education Pays."

The tech industry blames its poor diversity on too few women and minorities entering the tech industry, not on its own hiring practices. Facebook's head of Diversity Maxine Williams said in a statement "Appropriate representation in technology or any other industry will depend upon more people having the opportunity to gain the necessary skills through the public education system" As Open MIC notes in its report, **Breaking the Mold**, "Black people and Latinxs now earn nearly 18% of computer science degrees, but still hold barely 5% percent of tech jobs. For people of color, the 'right' education and credentials are no guarantee of a job" People of color are in the pipeline, but they aren't being hired. Most major tech companies look at only a very limited slice of that pipeline: graduates from Stanford, UC Berkeley. Even if Blacks graduate from these institutions, Blacks are still not hired as White tech leaders, unconsciously, believe American Blacks are not intelligent enough to work in the industry.

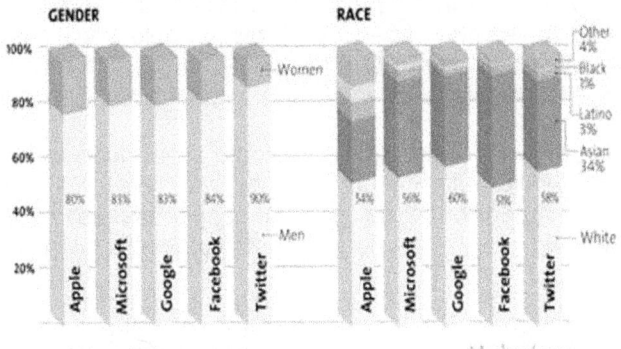

The creative tech industry desires employees with inventive creativity and technological expertise. Sadly, Black students noted in the 2009 Lemelson- MIT study that they know they are not prepared well for technology or inventing careers. Should more Blacks matriculate into STEM (Science, Technology Engineering and Mathematics) post-secondary training? Absolutely. It is easier said then done as Blacks have endured generations of servitude that forbade learning, diluted STEM secondary school curriculum and excessive intelligence testing to prove their inferiority.

Forbidden learning

Blacks learned hands-on skilled knowledge in carpentry, Blacksmith/ welding, mechanics, midwifery/ nursing and culinary arts, to power the agricultural revolution. Their knowledge and creativity led to patented inventions in the Industrial Revolution. Rather than embrace their intelligence Whites sought to disqualify them from acquiring the plethora of skilled trades jobs the Industrial Revolution created. Whites exploited Blacks greatest weakness - **INTELLIGENCE TEST**. Even into 2017, Blacks still have difficulty entering skilled trade professions.

Imagine relocating to Tokyo, and your family were forbidden to read or write Japanese. Imagine the horror if you and your family remained in Tokyo for 300 years and you never had Japanese classes. Could you pass an intelligence exam (IQ test) written in Japanese without ever studied read or written the language?

Could you matriculate to study at a postsecondary institution that requires you to have in-depth comprehension skills in a language you have never studied? That is the very existence of Blacks in America.

Black slaves were legally forbidden to read, and write as slave-owners believed "the teaching of slaves to read and write, has a tendency to excite dis-satisfaction in their minds, and to produce insurrection and rebellion," disrupting the operation of plantations." The first anti-slave education law was passed in 1740 in South Carolina in response to the Stono Rebellion where Jemmy on September 9, 1739 led the largest slave uprising in the British mainland colonies where 42-47 Whites and 44 Blacks were killed. Jemmy was considered a literate slave having spoken Portuguese. He recruited 60 slaves to fight for their freedom. Plantation owners needed to restrict slaves' ability to communicate with one another, read with abolitionist materials, forge passes, and plan another uprising. These laws became more restrictive in 1831 after Nate Turner killed 55-65 Whites in the Virginia revolt. Anyone caught teaching slaves to read were fined, beaten with at least 20 -39 lashes, jailed or even lynched.

While slavery ended in 1865, many Blacks never learned how to read and write as they were employed by plantations that restricted their ability to secure education as a condition of their 'NEW" labor contracts. Eventually the Freedman's Bureau assisted in the development of Black free schools, except many local districts refused to pay for secondary school as it interrupted the ability of young people 10 and older to work in sharecropping or domestic work.

Diluted Curriculum
While American education was initially created to groom American leadership for government and business, it found a new purpose in 1864- creation of a tolerant, civilized society. Horace Mann imported the Prussian system of schooling intended to teach minimal literacy, absolute obedience and uniformity. After the Civil War, this schooling began to replace the one room schoolhouse.

The Industrial Revolution needed workers to follow orders without thought. Horace Mann brokered a deal with corporate leaders to provide them the most compliant employees in exchange for them paying a tax to prepare these students. This new schooling model insured this process. Unlike the one room schoolhouse that integrated learning with industrial trade lessons, this school model divided the subjects to confuse the masses. It, also, limited the teaching of reading. Rather than teach Greek, Latin and etymology to expand comprehension and understanding, it focused on phonics, memorization and basic computation. This dilution was extended even further in the Black community as teachers taught the whole language reading instruction. Rote memorization of words, through 1980 even after the research showed it did not teach children to read.

The education of Blacks was to further those skills needed to fit the subservient needs of the White economy and society. Booker T. Washington reflected on the situation when he said in 1915 that "White men will vote funds for Negro education just in proportion to their belief in the value of that education." The only value to a White landowner ... lay in their ability to pick cotton or wash laundry. Any education beyond the rudiments of literacy and figuring would not only be wasted on them, but it might encourage them to seek higher education, which would make them unfit for working on White-owned farms and in White homes." In the Agricultural Revolution, six of every 10 Blacks labored on farms, and 3 in 10 Blacks, mostly women, worked in domestic service as cooks, housekeepers, laundresses, and nursemaids for White children. In the Industrial Revolution the men performed the manual task of iron ore/ glass pouring and assembly production.

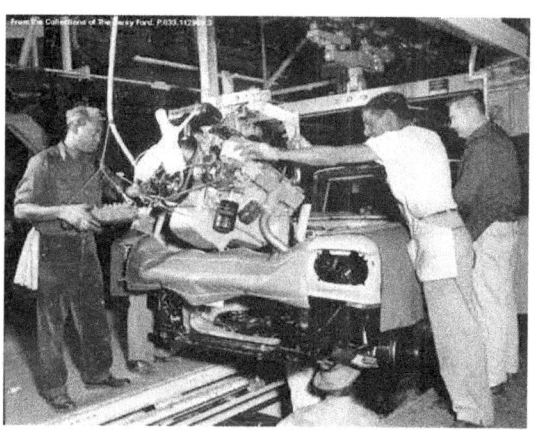

In 1932, only 14 percent of Blacks between 15 and 19 years old were enrolled in public secondary schools. A report on secondary education for Blacks in 1933 showed that between them, the states of Florida, Louisiana, Mississippi, and South Carolina had a total of 16 Black high schools accredited for four-year study. This report also noted that "89 percent of all Negro secondary schools are essentially elementary schools. The four-year high schools had few resources lacking science laboratories, foreign languages, music, or art. Their curriculum was limited and their teachers had little training in academic subjects.

The funding disparities in the Deep South states, where Blacks outnumbered Whites in hundreds of rural countries, were far greater. Alabama spent $37 on each White child in 1930 and just $7 on those who were Black; in Georgia the figures were $32 and $7, Mississippi they were $31 and $6, and those in South Carolina were $53 and $5, a disparity of more than 10-to-one. These funding disparities were not just in the Southern Jim Crow states, they occurred in Northern states as well. Schools were separate but certainly not equal then or even now.

College admissions exams are IQ Test
Mathematics, the universal language, is the new battleground for jobs. Mathematics is not just a computation. It is a problem solving process that includes logic, pattern recognition, visualization, spatial reasoning and deciphering of vocabulary to determine what computation gets to the desired answer.

Logic is defined by Merriam-Webster's dictionary as the science of the formal principles of reasoning- the drawing of inferences or conclusions. Who determines the validity of reason? It is determined by social mores, culture and general belief. For centuries, people thought the world was flat. If a person stated it was round, they were considered not logical until scientist proved the world is round. Reasoning, logic and mathematics is based on generally accepted facts and hence so is intelligence.

Intelligence (IQ) test and admissions exams measure a person's understanding of advanced theoretical and abstract facts in verbal, math, logic, pattern recognition, visualization, spatial reasoning. They are, in essence, test of reason. IQ test were created in 1905 initially to test mental retardation. The Army utilized intelligence test in World War I (WWI) to select officers. Army Alpha was a group-administered test that measured verbal ability, numerical ability, ability to follow directions, and knowledge of information. The Army Beta was a non-verbal counterpart to the Army Alpha. It was used to evaluate the aptitude of illiterate, unschooled, or non-English speaking draftees and volunteers. These test weeded out feebleminded soldiers. IQ test, still, do the same today. Score low and a person is eliminated from a plethora of opportunities.

The IQ test worked so well, College Entrance Examination Board combined it with subject matter questions to create the Scholastic Aptitude Test (SAT) as an admission exam for Northeastern Universities. A competitor, American College Testing (ACT) raced to distribute test to Midwestern and Southern colleges. Both test have questions of subject matter Blacks had not covered, despite schools across the country having Common Core standards. Often, Black students have only covered 50% of the required standards per year. If that happens every year, Black students would only cover 6.5 years of subject matter over a 13 year period. In essence, their high school curriculum is equivalent to elementary school making it difficult to solve a basic math word problem. Here is a sample question on a standardized test to gauge who is qualified to invent and create.

A car averages 27 miles per gallon. If gas costs $4.04 per gallon, which of the following is closest to how much the gas would cost for this car to travel 2,727 typical miles?

A $44.44
B $109.08
C $118.80
D $408.04
E $444.40

The correct answer is:
E. $444.40

Every time Blacks score low on an exam, it is publicized that schools are failing which is the code word, "Blacks, you are inferior." This perception was accelerated with No Child Left Behind (NCLB) every year from 2001 to 2016. An entire generation of students have heard they are failures for their entire academic history, which becomes a self-fulfilling prophecy. Schools were required to make adequate yearly progress. How can a student make yearly progress when they only cover 50% of the required curriculum standards? STEM classes are cumulative. If

Blacks are only receiving 50% of the instruction according to the standards, they would have a difficult time catching up on the basics in an apprenticeship, college or university level, causing their high dropout rates at this post-secondary level.

The curriculum dilution of the 1930s Black secondary school has been replicated in the 2000s weakening the ability of Blacks to score well on college admission/ standardized exams, matriculate to post-secondary training and secure high paying jobs and hence impairing their ability to collectively accumulate wealth and thus solidifying the notion – the Black community is inferior.

Chapter 6

Blacks Driving Mobile Tech Usage

The tech industry implies Blacks are not savvy enough to work for them but they even attempt to imply Blacks do not utilize their products.

Uplift, Inc., a nonprofit tech diversity & inclusion firm issued a survey of 25 questions to the 900 plus registrants of Automation Workz, a hands-on iSTEAM (invention, Science, Technology, Engineering, Arts and Mathematics) scavenger hunt, powered by a mobile app, held at the North American International Auto Show January 21, 2017 where families scurried from exhibit to exhibit completing activities to score points to win cash prizes. These activities use sponsor parts/digital services, toys, robots, computer coding, gaming, and puzzles as physical representation of mathematical standardized exam questions. These families, solved math, robotic and computer programming assignments in a fast paced competition to win cash prizes.

Ethnic Heritage Demographics Automation Workz Family Leaders ethnic heritage demographics.

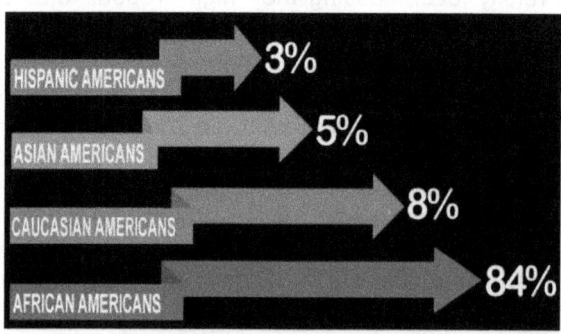

Automation Workz ethnic demographics data is similar to the City of Detroit population data statistics signifying this demographic data is a representative **Mobile Profile of the Native Detroiter** and hence inner city residents across America.

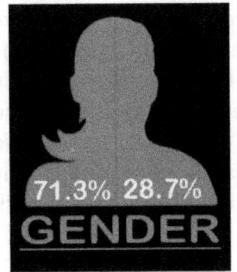

Native Detroiters surveyed 71.3% female Adults and 28.7% male Adults with 52.76% male children and 47.26% female children. Typical high-tech middle and high school events are predominately attended by male children. Ironically, 61% of Automation Workz children are not involved in DAPCEP (Detroit Area Pre-College Engineering Program) and neither are 86.8% involved in First Robotics.

These family leaders with children ranged in age from 15 to 75. Many of our teenagers have birthed children. Approximately, 57% of registrants were in the 35-54 age range slightly double their 25.23% representation within the City of Detroit population. These family leaders comprise the forgotten Generation Xers (Gen Xers).

Gen Xers were born between 1965 and 1981. They are the children of baby boomers. Gen Xers are the most misunderstood population.

Gen Xers are more ethnically diverse than Baby Boomers. According to the US Census Bureau America had 1% of multicultural babies born in 1970. In 2013, it was 10%. In Detroit specific 2.8% of the population indicated they were some other race than the top 5 while 2.1% indicated they were multiracial. Black Gen Xers attended college as Detroit's percentage of population with a Bachelor's degree increased to 12.1% and those who are multiracial increased to 24.9%. Gen Xers came of age in an era of two-income families, rising divorce rates, rising technology and a faltering economy. As a result, Gen Xers are independent, resourceful, and self-sufficient as they were "latch-key" children. They value freedom and responsibility. Many in this generation display a casual disdain for authority and structure.

Gen Xers work to live rather than lives to work. They love their families, birthing more children than their baby boomer parents. They are extremely frugal. Many live in urban settings as housing is cheaper and the dense structure of cities allow them to utilize public transportation. As of 2010, their assets were statistically double their debts even higher than the frugal 1929 depression era babies.

While the Gen Xers population is smaller than both the baby boomers and millennials, they as a group have caused silent seismic waves in business and in neighborhoods causing American companies and municipalities to either go BOOM or BUST.

Gen Xers are tech savvy, having grown up with the personal computer, video games and mobile phones. The tech industry is led by Gen Xers, who are disrupting every industry in the world. They have created products for their fellow Gen Xers and their families. They should be affectionately named 'Global Disruptors.' They disrupted and are still disrupting the American Automotive industry, headquartered in Detroit, purchasing the largest segment of foreign cars. They are driven by frugality and long term value. GM owes its drop in market share to Gen Xers. They ignored them and hence Gen Xers responded in kind. As they have aged, the market share declined even further. People of color are driving lots of Toyotas, Hondas, Kias, Hyundais, Volkswagens, BMWs and Mercedes etc. They have abandoned American auto companies, cities and traditional public schools in droves.

The data per category does not add up to 100% in most cases as Gen Xers are flexible brand loyalist.

Meaning they support a multiplicity of competing brands simultaneously.

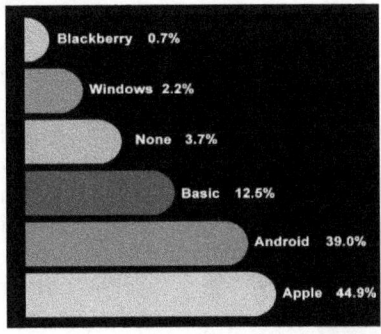

The mobile phone has closed the digital divide - the gulf between those who have ready access to computers and the Internet, and those who do not. Joan Ganz Cooney Center at Sesame Workshop completed research in 2015 that shows 85 percent of families living below the poverty line have some kind of digital device, smartphone or tablet, in their household. Approximately 73% have one or more smartphones, compared to 84 percent for families above the poverty line. This data has changed significantly, since 2011 in a study commissioned by Common Sense that highlighted households under $30,000 income with children, only 27 percent of them had a smartphone, compared to 57 percent for households with children and income over $75,000.

The first mobile phone went on sale in 1983, meaning these Gen Xers have been exposed to mobile phones for 34 years. Approximately, 96.3% of Native Detroiters own a cellphone and 86.8% own a smart phone. The mobile phone is a necessary tool for these Gen Xer parents albeit many do not own desktop or laptop computers. The mobile phone industry is benefitting from Gen Xers obsession with technology. Americans went from 1-2 home landlines to 1-4 mobile phones for everyone in the household. A family can buy a good quality Android phone for $40 dollars whereas a laptop would cost $300 and a desktop computer $600. For those who are in poverty, they can get a phone for free. Interesting to note: Few household were 100% loyal to Android, IOS, Windows or Basic operating systems. It appears many households have a multiplicity of phone brands they use simultaneously.

These parents have a combination of traditional, prepaid and lifeline mobile carriers within their household. Traditional carriers have a 2 year contract period. Prepaid carriers have no contract and operates as the bill is paid. Lifeline carriers provide free phones to qualified low income residents as a FCC program subsidy. The top five carriers comprise 1 prepaid carrier

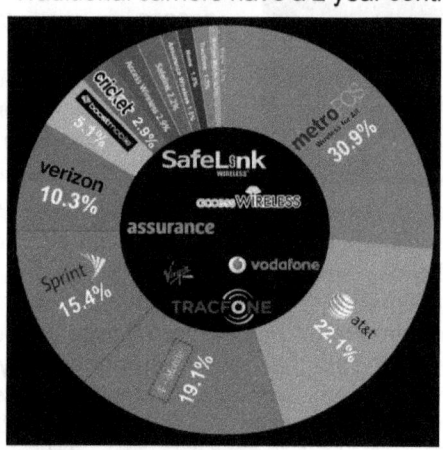

- MetroPCs with 30.9% share, and 4 traditional carriers - AT&T, 22.1% share, T-Mobile 19.1% share, Sprint 15.4%, Verizon 10.3% totaling 97.8%. The remaining mobile phone carriers utilized are prepaid and lifeline carriers totaling 17.5%.

Phone manufacturers Apple and Samsung have benefitted from Gen Xers and people of color. In fact, they are the two leading phone brands noted with 39.7% owning Samsung phones and 29.6% owning iPhones. LG was number 3 with 17.6%. While most

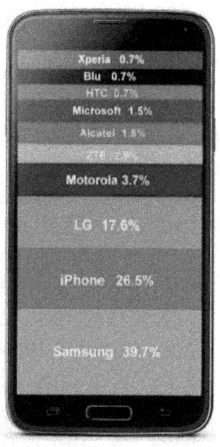

INVISIBLE TALENT MARKET 64

indicated their dominate phone operating system earlier in the survey was Apple we discovered they had multiple types of phones in their home with the Android mainly distributed to their children as the price was a lot lower than iPhone.

Family leaders utilize their phones for multiplicity of purposes:

1. Improve their productivity
2. Manage their finances.
3. Search for jobs
4. Secure directions
5. Arrange transportation options
6. Shop
7. Interact with family and friends
8. Listen to music
9. View videos
10. Play video games

1.   IMPROVE THEIR PRODUCTIVITY

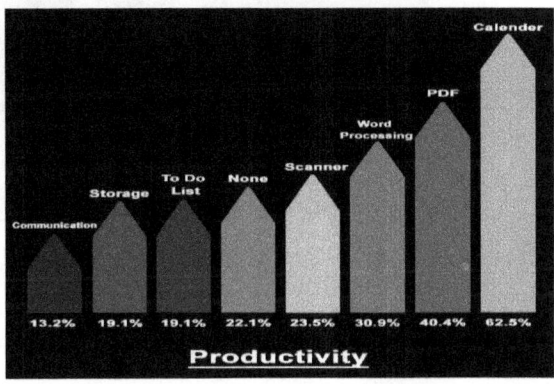

Native Detroiters utilize their mobile phone as mini computers - 62.5% set up meetings and family deadlines on their calendar; 40.4% read PDF files; 30.9% Type documents utilizing word processing software; 23.5% scan documents; 19.1% manage tasks with a to-do list; 19.1% store documents electronically and 13.2% communicate through instant messaging platforms.

2. MANAGE THEIR FINANCES

Banking Relationships

Many Native Detroiter maintain relationships with 2 or more financial institutions. Adult Native Detroiter appears to have little loyalty collectively to financial institutions as they utilize 25 different financial institutions. The top financial institutions are Chase and Michigan First Credit

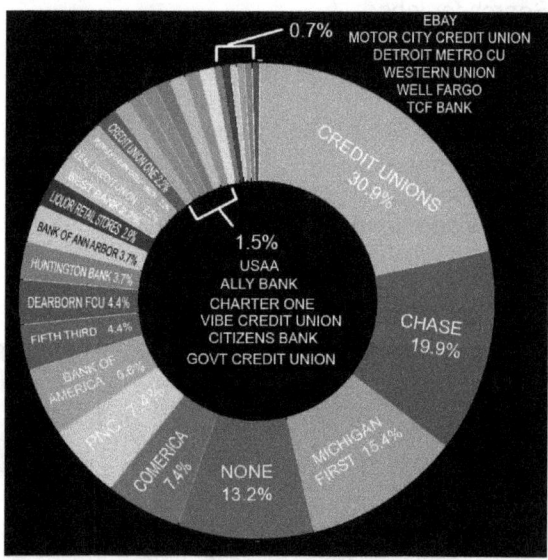

Union with 19.9% and 15.4% respectively. Even with such financial diversity 13.2% have no banking relationship at all and 2.9% utilize check cashing as well as their primary bank relationship.

Individuals are considered unbanked if they have no banking relationship at all and underbanked if they utilize prepaid debit cards, Money transfer, check cashing and in addition to their banking accounts CFED highlights in the unbanked and underbanked reports that 20% of the

Detroit population is considered unbanked and of 29.8% underbanked. Our data shows the Native Detroiters in our survey as 16.1% unbanked is and 30.1% underbanked.

Prepaid Debit Cards

While 69.9% of adult Native Detroiters do not own prepaid debit cards, the remaining 30.1% own several prepaid debit cards. American Express 15.4% Netspend, 14.7% and Green Dot 11% are primarily used albeit American Express is used under the brand name of Walmart Bluebird and Serve.

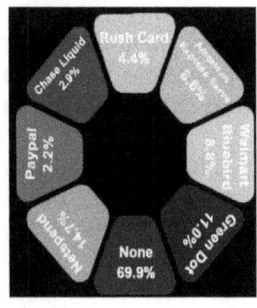

Favorite Financial Apps

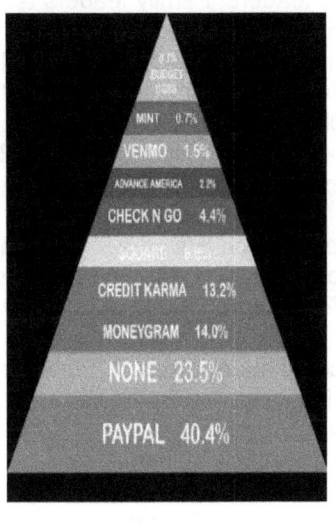

Native Detroiters have various favorite financial apps:

48.5% are payment providers – PayPal, Square and Venmo;

14% are money transfer agents – MoneyGram

13.2% are credit score educators– Credit Karma

6.6% are check cashers – Advance America, Check N Go;

1.4% are budget – Mint and Budget Boss

Credit Karma advertises heavily on Bounce TV, an African American broadcast network televised on channel 7.2 illustrating adult Native Detroiters desire to improve their credit and purchasing power.

3. SEARCH FOR CAREER ADVANCEMENT

Carl Jung states "***Nothing has a stronger influence psychologically on their environment and especially on their children than the unlived life of a parent.***"

"***Children have never been very good at listening to their elders, but they have never failed to imitate them.***" states James Baldwin.

Children often follow in their family leader's career choices and aspirations as they are able to hear and experience their parents' successes and regrets. To move children to a higher level of success requires improving the career options of family leaders. Family leaders tend to hover over their children to fulfill the requirements they were unable to complete. If the family leader was unable to finish high school they desire for their children to finish. If they aspired to attend college and was unable to do so, they desire for their children to do so. Approximately 83% of our family leaders had job titles they aspire to achieve.

Adult Native Detroiters aspire to achieve career goals in: **Business Services** to become Project Coordinators, Operation Managers and Procurement buyers.

Engineering seeking to complete degrees in Electrical, Mechanical, Mechatronic, Robotics and Software.

Entrepreneurship across a plethora of industries.

Education in both pk-12, higher Ed and corporate training as administrators, Instructional Specialist, Teachers and Professor

Medical Science to become Registered nurse (RN), orthodontist, Physician Assistant, Physician.

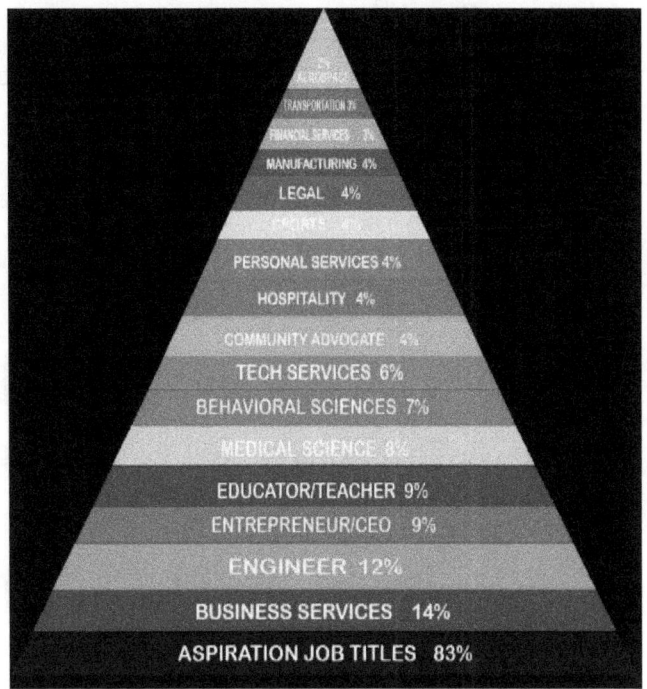

Behavioral Science to achieve careers as Clinical Instructor, Clinical Therapist, counselor, Program Manager, Psychologist or Social Work.

Tech Services education to secure positions in computer & cellphone programmers, Cyber Security Specialist, Programmer, Video game designer, Software Developer.

Manufacturing as a CNC Operator, Metals Recyclist, and Chemist.

Legal professions as a Lawyer, Legal Assistant, Real Estate Lawyer.

Financial Services as an Accountant, Banker, Financial Consultant

Job/ Career Search App
Only 27.9% of Native Detroiters do not have a favorite Job/Career app, meaning 72.1% are looking for new job opportunities. Indeed leads the path with 30.9% usage with Career Builder and Linked In a distant 2nd and 3rd. Only 22.1% utilize Linked In as social media option, but 25% utilize LinkedIn as Job/Career Search site. Michigan Talent Bank is utilized more than Monster and Zip Recruiter. The most popular sites are more mobile responsive than others.

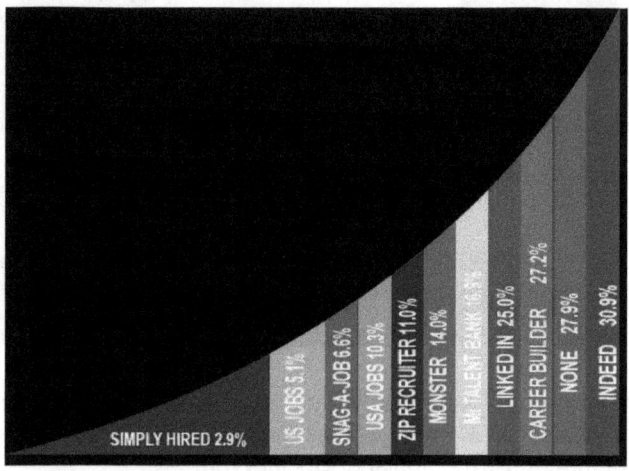

4. SECURE DIRECTIONS

Native Detroiters utilize multiple map apps with 76% choosing Google Maps as the leading favorite, even for those who own phones with IOS, Blackberry and windows operating systems.

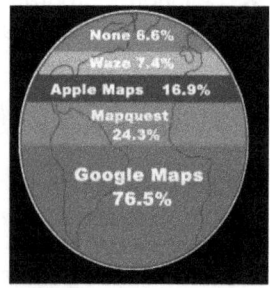

5. ARRANGE TRANSPORTATION OPTIONS

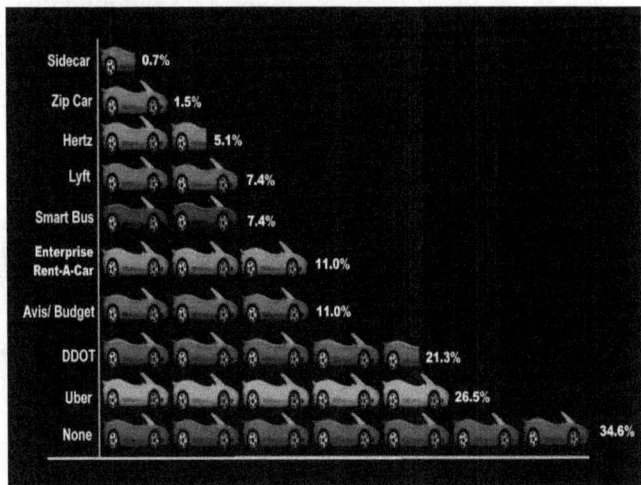

It appears those with no or limited transportation options is driving diverse mobility options. Uber is the leading Mobility app with 26.5% usage followed by DDOT 21.03%, Avis/Budget 11% and Enterprise Rent-A-Car 11% Smart Bus 7.4% Lyft 7.4%. Native Detroiter are utilizing Uber/Lyft on-demand private taxi service, DDOT/Smart Bus mass transit and rental car. Ironically Native Detroiters are barely utilizing Zip car, a blend of on demand car service and rental agency.

6. SHOP

There is limited brand name and luxury shopping within the City of Detroit. While Native Detroiters commute to shopping malls in neighboring counties, many Native Detroiters have become loyal to various online shopping sites Amazon leads the

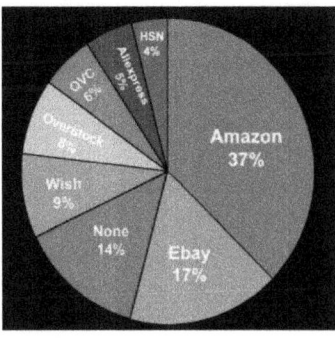

INVISIBLE TALENT MARKET 71

way capturing 61.8% of Native Detroiters surveyed followed by EBay Wish. Ali Express headquartered in China made the list with 8.8% usage. Online shopping drives the growth of domestic and international shippers. FedEx, UPS, USPS and DHL as seen daily in Detroit neighborhoods delivering packages

7. INTERACT WITH FAMILY AND FRIENDS

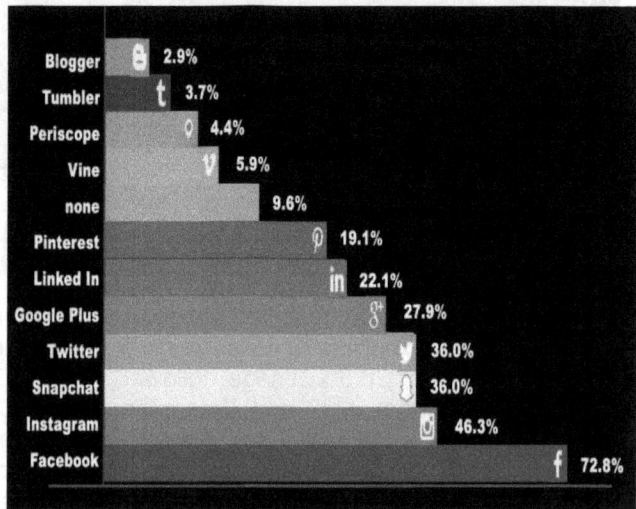

Facebook is the dominate social media site utilized by Native Detroiters. While Native Detroiters have chosen Facebook the oldest remaining social media company, they are early adopters of other social media. Number 2 and 3 are Instagram and Snapchat. The second oldest social media company, Twitter is a distant 4th. Native Detroiters have embraced Google +, LinkedIn, Periscope, Pinterest and Vine. There are a few who blog utilizing Tumblr and Blogger.

8. LISTEN TO MUSIC

Native Detroiters love music utilizing 16 different music apps. YouTube and Pandora are slugging it out for dominance as 71.3% utilize YouTube, a video site, for their music and 69.9% utilize Pandora. The second tier apps are Spotify, Google Play, iHeart and Sound cloud.

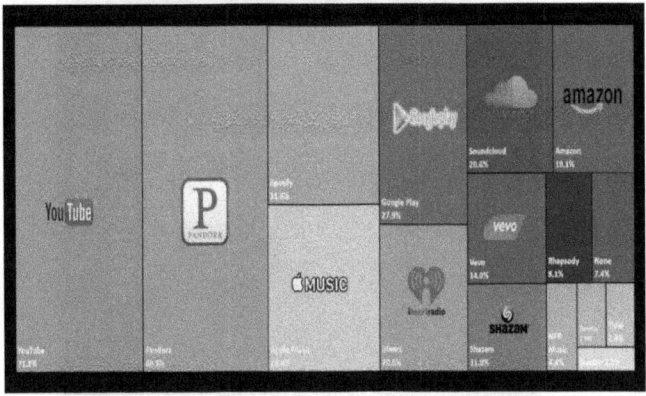

9.   **VIEW VIDEOS**

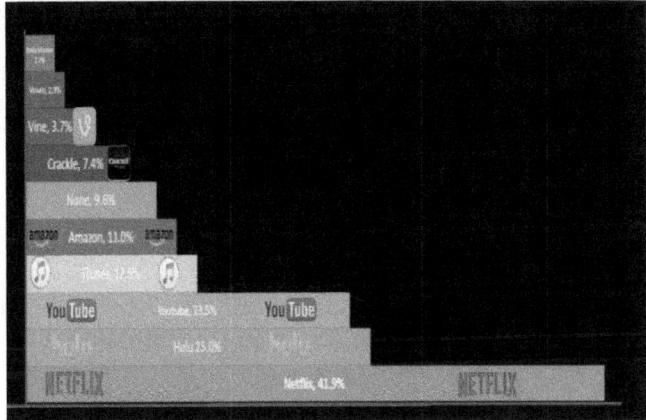

YouTube leads in the music category but is a distant third in the video category behind Netflix and Hulu. These cord cutters prefer Netflix with 41.9% usage compared to Hulu 25% and YouTube 23.5%. Surprising choices - Crackle with 7.4% usage and Daily Motion with 2.2% usage

10. PLAY VIDEO GAMES

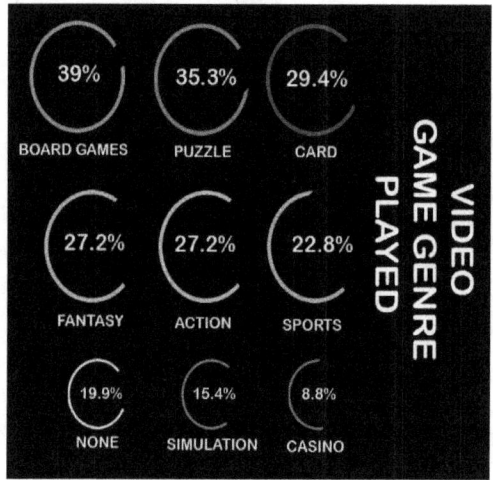

People of color Gen Xers propelled the video game industry to new revenue heights as they dominate revenue in the mobile video game space. African Americans followed by Hispanics spent more money on video games. Even during the 2008 recession the video game industry did not suffer a downturn. Ironically, people of color are playing every video game genre.

Game Genre	Sample Game
Board Games	Scrabble, Yahtzee
Puzzle	Candy Crush, Toy Blast
Card	Poker, Spades,
Fantasy	Pokémon Go, Subway Surfer, Marvel
Action	Clash of Clans
Sports	NBA Live, Madden NFL
Simulation	Sims, Cooking Fever
Casino	777 slot machines

Board games, puzzles and card games dominate followed by Fantasy, Action Sports, Simulation and Casino. Ironically board games, puzzles and cards teach strategy, critical thinking and number counting, the precursor to problem solving and mathematics. Blacks struggle with Mathematics proficiency on standardized exams yet they naturally choose the most popular game genres that are the foundation for mathematics. Native Detroiters are not loyal to a specific genre as they play multiple genres in their household.

Urban cities are characterized as digital deserts. While this population lacks desktop computers, Native Detroiters are quite consumer tech savvy, thanks to the mobile smart phone, their "computer of choice." This means their millennial and generation Z children are even more tech savvy. In fact, when we operated Hustle & TECHknow Preparatory High School (H&T), an alternative high school located in the Compuware headquarters, we discovered these students –millennials- had a "Consumer *Technology Obsession*" just like the family leaders in this profile.

Tech companies of all types automotive, consumer, financial, healthcare and retail have grown wildly due to Blacks nationwide utilizing their products, yet these companies hire mainly affluent White individuals, test their products in White affluent communities, and place their sales offices in the same White affluent communities.

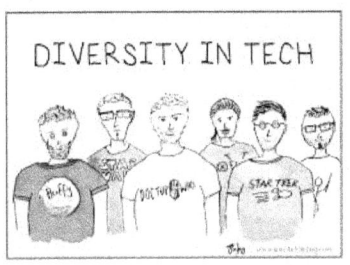

The Black community is mobile connected. They will no longer be ignored, invisible or insignificant. Detroit is a microcosm of the projected population shift of 2044 when people of color will become the majority population. Detroit is the perfect place to experiment and invent new products to prepare for this demographic shift.

Chapter 7

Underserved = Economic Profit

"The advantage that countries like the United States retain is the ability to invent – to dream up solutions to problems that people may not yet even know they have."
Dr. Stuart Brown, Author, **Play**
Professor, Stanford D. School

Blacks have been a creative inventive people for centuries. Blacks have invented and even patented inventions throughout the Industrial Revolution. Today they have invented the culture of 'cool'. They have been the foundation for fashion and entertainment - video gaming, both console and mobile, movies, weekly sitcoms/ dramas. Electronic Arts, Xbox Candy Crush, and Game Stop have benefitted from their video game craze. Blacks have accelerated the rapid adoption of smartphones – mini-computer. Metro PCS, AT&T, Sprint, Samsung, Apple and LG are growing as Blacks purchase new phones every 2 years. Blacks are driving the growth of urban mobility, as they are the majority population in inner cities. Uber and Lyft caters to urban residents who struggle with transportation issues in securing a taxicab or reliable bus transportation. These are mainly people of color - African, Hispanic, and Native Americans residents, who do not own a car. We celebrate the startups who earn money from people of color customers, but not the customer. People of color are definitely an underserved market flush with cash.

Black buying power is projected to reach $1.2 trillion this year and $1.4 trillion by 2020, according to a report from the University of Georgia's Selig Center for Economic Growth. That's 275 percent growth since 1990, when black buying power was $320 billion. Already black consumers represent the largest consumers of color

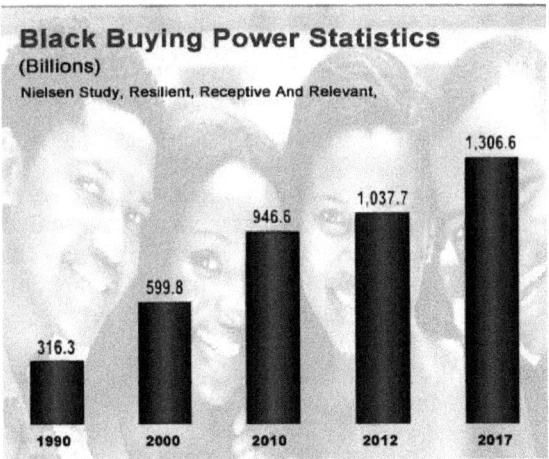

Black Buying Power Statistics
(Billions)
Nielsen Study, Resilient, Receptive And Relevant,

- 1990: 316.3
- 2000: 599.8
- 2010: 946.6
- 2012: 1,037.7
- 2017: 1,306.6

group in the marketplace, the report shows. Yet, Blacks have been an underserved market in America for decades as racism prevented mainstream corporate leaders from seeing them as valuable. The term, underserved, in marketing and economics, is a market that is ignored where needs are not met. Underserved markets are the true definition of economic profit where demand (needs) is higher than supply.

In the midst of White America openly expressing their hatred of Blacks, torturing them throughout history, the Black community produced entrepreneurs, who served their needs. Blacks created stores, consulting firms, hotels, business service firms, cosmetics, newspapers, music production etc. spending their dollars amongst each other. Blacks created prosperous neighborhoods like Greenwood of Tulsa OK, Rosewood, FL and Paradise Valley of Detroit, MI. Many Civil Right gains came from collective consumer activism forged during segregation. Blacks carved their place in America by limiting their spending to Black businesses or businesses that supported their success. At the same time, integration became possible, riots, spurred by pure racists actions, decimated many Black communities. Black affluent and middle class residents moved to White suburban communities to shop and live. Street civil protests disappeared, giving the illusion of success. While Blacks have annual income exceeding 1.2 trillion dollars, larger than the Gross Domestic product of Mexico, their business community has disappeared, except in key places, where Blacks are the majority population. The Black Enterprise Magazine 2016 100 top Black companies had 16 companies in DC Metro, 13 in Detroit Metro and 9 in Atlanta Metro.

Black Economic Power
Tired of being underserved in society, Blacks have begun to produce their own products and services in mass quantity. They have set the world ablaze in entertainment - movies, sitcoms and music-clothing, financial products, alcoholic beverages, auto designs supported by Blacks and now, mainstream America.

Shows and movies like Empire and Hidden figures are proving the economic profit of Blacks. Empire received a Nielsen rating of 5.9. A top show usually gets a rating of 2.7 to 3.0. People are seeing that shows with people of color can make money," Taraji P. Henson told reporters days after *Empire*'s second episode solidified its status as the highest-rated new series of the 2014-15 TV season. Hidden Figures finished number 1 at the box office ahead of Rogue One a Star Wars franchise 3 weeks in a row.

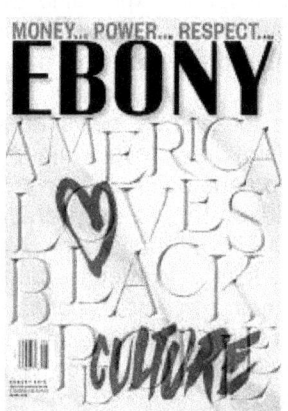

Despite the economic power of Blacks and their relative success, America hates Black people but loves its 'cool' culture. Ebony highlighted this dilemma on its cover for its August 2015 issue. Blacks have become more invisible to companies, especially digital tech companies, who have refused to employ them, contract with their companies as suppliers, or acknowledge them as customers as if they don't need Blacks. Today they may not. However, tomorrow they will.

People of color – Black, Arabic, Asian Hispanic and Native Americans - are projected to be the majority population in 2044, a short 27 years from 2017. Americans, afraid they will lose more jobs as this demographic population shift accelerates, elected Trump as President. His slogan "Make America great again" has been interpreted to mean a return to America in the 1940s-1960s when racial segregation was overt, locking Blacks out of jobs, with the belief that when Blacks get jobs Whites are losing jobs. **Computer programming is the skilled trades of 21st century**. Digital tech executives have resurrected the skill trades "freeze out" of the 1940-1960s where Whites vehemently committed violence to limit the entry of Blacks. They have resurrected the Black Brawn vs White Brains debate not realizing employment segregation is bad for business and bad for America.

Blacks have the power to increase and decrease brand popularity, and hence sales. In 2006 after Jay-Z was insulted by Fredric Rouzaud, Blacks stopped buying Cristal dropping its market share as Moet increased. Tommy Hilfiger and Liz Claiborne have watched their brands' value cheapen after mythical racist comments. In 2002, Adidas designed a men's shoe with an actual shackle in the age of mass incarceration  causing Blacks to abandon their shoes. Tech companies, growing exponentially, have not felt the pain of a Black boycott, yet. But know it is coming…… Nothing is going to stop this population shift. Not even a President with White supremacist employees and colleagues.

Companies with diverse employees are more profitable as they represent a companies' diverse client base with the ability to create products for this client base. A 35% increase is huge. To seize this profitable underserved market, Human Resources leaders must tie Human Resources directly to the corporate growth strategy by borrowing Supply Chain Management, Marketing and Financial Profitability concepts. These 4 actions can move corporations to '**SEE**' the Invisible Talent Market clearer.

I. **EMBRACE AND DIVERSITY AS A BUSINESS STRATEGY THAT IF IGNORED COULD RUIN YOUR BUSINESS.**

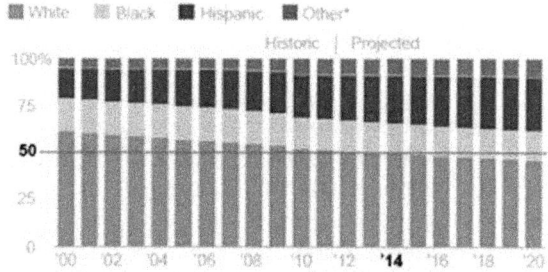

US PUBLIC SCHOOL DEMOGRAPHIC PROJECTIONS

Public school enrollment by year

*Includes Asian/Pacific Islander, American Indian/Alaska Native and, starting in 2008, people of two or more races.

SOURCE: National Center for Education Statistics

The US Public School System is an example of the damage that would occur if America ignores this demographic shift. In 2014, people of color became the majority of students in public schools, 50.3% of the population. Educational Leaders knew this shift was happening but failed to diversify the teaching staff, retool the curriculum to match the learning styles of students of color or immerse staff in cultural diversity/ cultural awareness training.

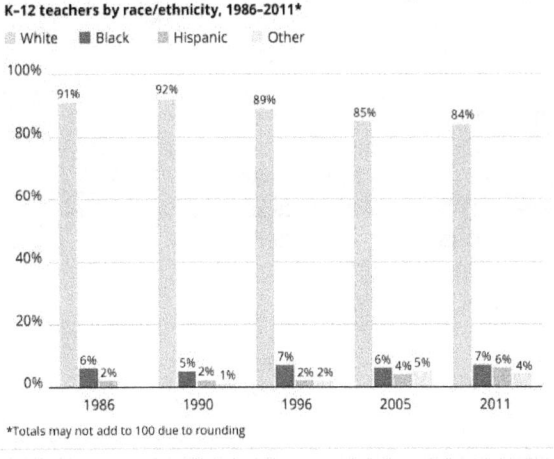

Teachers Are Still Overwhelmingly White

K-12 teachers by race/ethnicity, 1986-2011*

*Totals may not add to 100 due to rounding

Source: National Center for Education Information — THE HUFFINGTON POST

While 50% of students are diverse, the teaching staff of US public schools is still 84% White. Educational leaders, knowing racial bias has been full-blown in schools for decades, failed to protect students and America's talent pipeline. This racial bias continues through elementary, middle and high school. A John Hopkins research study **Teachers Predictions** asked two different teachers, who each taught a particular student in either math or reading, to predict how far that one student would go in school. With White students, the ratings from both teachers tended to be the same. But with Black students, boys in particular, there were big differences — the White teachers had much lower expectations than Black teachers for how far the Black students would go in school. When a Black teacher and a White teacher evaluate the same Black student, the White teacher is about 30 percent less likely to predict the student will complete a four-year college degree. White teachers are also almost 40 percent less likely to expect their Black students will graduate high school. "What we find is that White teachers and Black teachers systematically disagree about the exact same student," said co-author Nicholas Papageorge, an economist in the Krieger School of Arts and Science. For Black students, particularly Black boys, having a non-Black teacher in a 10th grade subject made them much less likely to pursue specialization in that subject by enrolling in similar classes. This suggests biased expectations by teachers have long-term effects on student outcomes, the researchers said. America is living with this long-term effect as most math and science high school teachers are White and they are disengaging Blacks from these subjects. In another John Hopkins University study, **The Long-Run Impacts of Same-Race Teachers, published** Having at least one Black teacher in third through fifth grades reduced a Black student's probability of dropping out of school by 29 percent. For very low-income Black boys, the results are even greater – their chance of dropping out fell 39 percent. In a study published in the Child Development journal, it shows that when Black and Latino middle school students notice racial

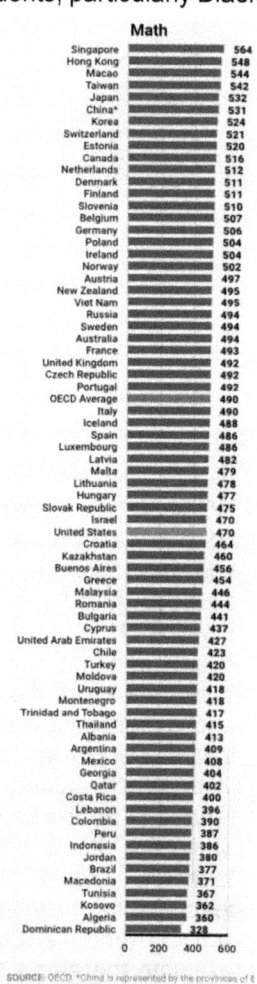

Math

Country	Score
Singapore	564
Hong Kong	548
Macao	544
Taiwan	542
Japan	532
China*	531
Korea	524
Switzerland	521
Estonia	520
Canada	516
Netherlands	512
Denmark	511
Finland	511
Slovenia	510
Belgium	507
Germany	506
Poland	504
Ireland	504
Norway	502
Austria	497
New Zealand	495
Viet Nam	495
Russia	494
Sweden	494
Australia	494
France	493
United Kingdom	492
Czech Republic	492
Portugal	492
OECD Average	490
Italy	490
Iceland	488
Spain	486
Luxembourg	486
Latvia	482
Malta	479
Lithuania	478
Hungary	477
Slovak Republic	475
Israel	470
United States	470
Croatia	464
Kazakhstan	460
Buenos Aires	456
Greece	454
Malaysia	446
Romania	444
Bulgaria	441
Cyprus	437
United Arab Emirates	427
Chile	423
Turkey	420
Moldova	420
Uruguay	418
Montenegro	418
Trinidad and Tobago	417
Thailand	415
Albania	413
Argentina	409
Mexico	408
Georgia	404
Qatar	402
Costa Rica	400
Lebanon	396
Colombia	390
Peru	387
Indonesia	386
Jordan	380
Brazil	377
Macedonia	371
Tunisia	367
Kosovo	362
Algeria	360
Dominican Republic	328

SOURCE: OECD *China is represented by the provinces of B

bias at school, they are more likely to lose trust in their teachers and other authority figures. Among Black students, when their trust in school declined, their rate of college enrollment was about 43%, but when their trust increased, it was about 64%, said David Yeager, an assistant professor of developmental psychology at the University of Texas at Austin and lead author of the study. So, there was a difference of 21 percentage points. Instead of preparing students to master iSTEAM for the world of future technology and post-secondary training, educational leaders have been pipelining Black students for prison. Around the nation, **1.6 million kids** attended schools that have a law enforcement officer but no counselor. And Asian, Black and Latino students were more likely to be among those kids, which is why America ranks 41 out of 72 nations in Math on the 2015 PISA and 31 out of 35 on the 2012 Math PISA.

Black Unemployment and Underemployment
This racial bias has caused the proverbial talent shortage lessening America's competitiveness. It has caused high unemployment and underemployment in the Black community as young people have not been fully prepared for 21st century skilled jobs. The unemployment rate is a measure of those looking for work.

Unemployment rate of workers age 16 and older by race and ethnicity, 1973–2017

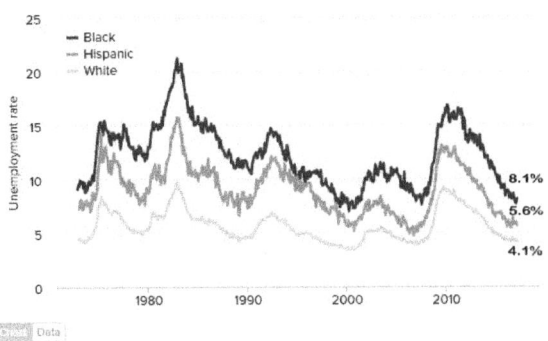

Source: Bureau of Labor Statistics' Current Population Survey, public data series

While the February 2017 unemployment rate for Whites is 4.1%, it is 8.1% for Blacks.

The underemployment rate is a measure of those looking for work plus those who have a part-time job but who are

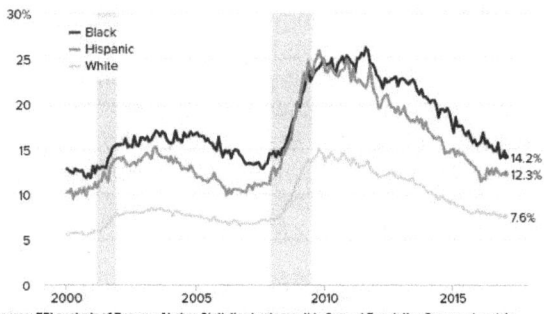

All races hurt by recession, racial and ethnic disparities persist
Underemployment rate of workers age 16 and older by race, 2000–2017

Source: EPI analysis of Bureau of Labor Statistics basic monthly Current Population Survey microdata

looking for a full time job. This rate is more important than the unemployment rate as it measures the strength of the economy based on full-time employment. Many people have gotten locked into part-time or gig jobs to make ends meet. The February 2017 underemployment rate for Whites is 7.6%, it is 14.2% for Blacks. Neither the unemployment or underemployment rates measure the full extent of joblessness as many people have stopped hunting for jobs altogether.

This joblessness has increased child poverty rate to astronomical rates. In Detroit child poverty has eclipsed 59%. If Educational leaders continue to ignore this people of color demographic shift, America will become the land of poverty. Companies need to get Blacks back to work. Jobs and skill credentials are changing so fast. High demand jobs in 1999 are obsolete in 2017. Some of the unemployment and underemployment of Blacks is due to weak skills. However, a lot of this dilemma is due to racial bias in the staffing process.

II. EMPLOY BLIND STAFFING STRATEGIES

DITCH the resume as the initial screening tool

The staffing process has been segmented to resemble a supply chain to simplify the process, and remove the bias.

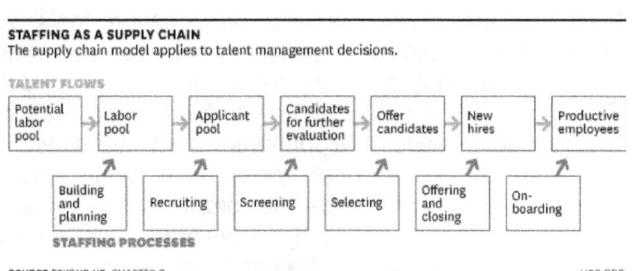

STAFFING AS A SUPPLY CHAIN
The supply chain model applies to talent management decisions.

SOURCE *BEYOND HR*, CHAPTER 7

The problem: The application, the starting point, is full of bias. The resume and EEOC/ Affirmative Action demographic data at the end of the application are tools that perpetuate bias. Every company begins the application process with a resume that auto-populates recruiting software. Resumes are summaries of an individual's credentials and experience. The talent shortage is a lack of skills to match the jobs in demand. CEOs are looking for skills, Oxford Dictionary defines skills as the ability to do something well. Most HR departments created job descriptions with specific credentials to document skills. Credentials and experiences are not skills.

National Bureau of Economic Research Faculty Research Fellows Marianne Bertrand and Sendhil Mullainathan completed a study, **Are Emily and Greg More Employable than Lakisha and Jamal? A Field Experiment on Labor Market Discrimination** showing people with ethnic names need to send out 50% more resumes before they get a callback than job hunters with

"White"-sounding names highlighting ethnic bias occurs. The same bias occurs with gender, education, age and social class. The resume is a tool of bias. I fired an employee who had collected the applications of the Black sounding names and removed them from the application pool. DITCH the resume as the initial screening tool.

Resumes are great interview presentation tools that should be collected after applicants have been screened for skills. Technology allows for the acquisition of data. Talent acquisition can move the staffing process from gut feelings and biases to algorithms. The initial screening tool should be a brief personality and aptitude assessment to categorize the problem solving skills individuals have beyond keywords, credentials, experiences and biases. Rather than categorizing the information by name, it can be categorized by email and candidate numbers to remove ethnic, gender, education, age, geographic and social class identifiers.

Then potential employees upload their resume into a recruiting database and answer EEOC Demographic/ Affirmative Action demographic data collection should be outsourced to an independent third party. In order to comply with Federal EEOC and Affirmative Action requirements, employer are required to collect <u>anonymous</u> demographic data on who applies for jobs, and/ or who is employed. Most companies collect this information at the end of each unique application so it is not anonymous. In theory, the information is not supposed to be utilized for screening. However most systems do not separate the information from the application once inputted. Information remains with the application providing opportunity for bias Corporations need to hire third parties to collect the information. Once it is entered, it should be hidden from everyone and dumped into a separate database that labels the information with a candidate number with no application identifiers.

Survey current employees to determine success profile and required skills to recruit for

Every company has top performers that if they were able to replicate their skills, the company would become more productive and profitable. Every company should know the success profile and skills for every top performer as this information should be the baseline for recruitment, staffing and professional development. This information could be. Often, companies attempt to replicate top performers by asking employees to send referrals hiring friends and relatives. Be systematic and data driven. Survey current employees to identify any skills and attributes that are common to the top performers, but missing from the other groups in the category. This concrete and specific profile can be utilized to build skill based job descriptions, create skills recruiting material and develop skills based training to assist the average and below average employee improve. With the focus on definable skills, bias and vagueness will be removed.

Analyze what bias your company is facing and how to playfully remove it

Sometimes bias can be simply hiring mostly White males or it can be hiring people born in the same social class. Analyze your employee base and compare it to your client base. Do they mirror each other? If not, bias is within your Human Resources System. Employees create products and services for your client base. How can they develop suitable products and services when they cannot relate to your client base? Software companies, automotive tech companies and social media companies are guilty of this dilemma. Of the Blacks who are internet users, 67% utilize Facebook, 47% utilize Instagram, 28% utilize Twitter 23% utilize Pinterest and 22% utilize Linked In. These National numbers are similar to the data regarding Native Detroiters. Mitigate your recruiting bias by focusing on skills and new geographic recruiting pools. Tech companies draw clients from all over the world and should draw employees the same way. Borrow from the Marketing Department's playbook. Engineer real competition with a playful contest. Plato states, "***You can learn more about a man in one hour of play than in a year of conversation***." Let applicants showcase their skills in an on-site or online contest. It can be live video game tournament, audition, hackathon or hands-on activity. Experiment with an online contest first. Create a video or problem solving contest for those who are currently in your applicant pool or open it up to the world and create a bigger pool. What is certain, individuals, who enter a contest that requires interaction and preparation, are an engaged audience. Let these contests lead the staffing process before selecting who to interview. Blacks are competitive as illustrated in Sports and music. Remove the barriers and let them compete freely. They have risen to the top when there are no barriers.

In 1970, Toronto Symphony Orchestra (TSO) was made up of almost all White male musicians. They changed, they changed their hiring tactics in 1980. When auditioning prospective members, they put a screen in front of the actual people who were looking to hire people so all they heard was the music that was being played. The orchestra moved to half-female, half-male, with more people of color," TSO got a brilliant result in terms of the sound they wanted for their orchestra and, at the same time, the diversity.
"

Recruit for Profitability, not 'Cultural Fit'
When diverse candidates amass credentials for digital jobs, they, then, have to deal with the newest form of bias – cultural fit. My son, who is an information 4th year technology student, was asked by a company to work 1 week for free to determine his "**cultural fit**." I requested they put the request in writing, which they refused to do.

It has been said "*Culture eats strategy for breakfast, technology for lunch, and products for dinner, and soon thereafter everything else too.*" The cliché is true, "But in many organizations, [cultural] fit has gone rogue," argued Lauren A. Rivera in a recent piece in *The New York*

Times. The associate professor of management and organizations at Northwestern University's Kellogg School of Management interviewed 120 decision makers, and found them deploying subjective personal criteria rather than screening for candidates who could thrive on established organizational values. "Bonding over rowing college crew, getting certified in scuba, sipping single-malt Scotches in the Highlands or dining at Michelin-starred restaurants was considered evidence of fit; sharing a love of teamwork or a passion for pleasing clients was not.

Culture is the DNA of a company. It is the vision, mission and values each company lives by. It is created by the founders – who define what is important to them to create value for their customers. Paul English, built a unique culture of action and accountability at Kayak. Decision making meetings had no more than three people. Everything from conference rooms to incentives plans evolved around this value. While the tradeoff was the lack of consensus, Kayak's revenue per employee was $1.25 million, more than double the industry average. In June 2013, Kayak was purchased for $1.8 billion by Priceline.com.

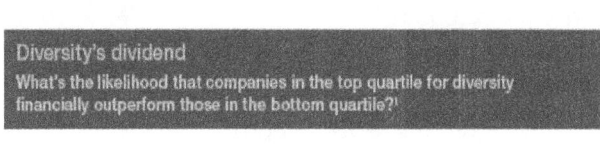

Diversity's dividend
What's the likelihood that companies in the top quartile for diversity financially outperform those in the bottom quartile?[1]

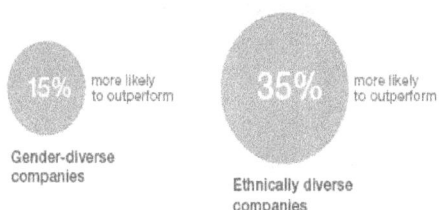

15% more likely to outperform — Gender-diverse companies

35% more likely to outperform — Ethnically diverse companies

[1]Results show likelihood of financial performance above the national industry median. Analysis is based on composite data for all countries in the data set. Results vary by individual country.

Source: McKinsey analysis

Homogenous work groups are not the highest performing teams. Companies with diverse employees are 35% more profitable as non-homogenous teams are simply smarter. Working with people who are different from you may challenge your brain to overcome its stale ways of thinking and sharpen its performance.

People assemble as work groups, but only become teams when they migrate through Tuckman's 5 stages of team development.

Those 5 stages are:

Forming is the initial stage and bond where people are extremely polite.

Storming is the stage where conflicts come to life whether in setting the direction for the team or possible jockeying to become leader of team.

Norming is the stage where the team resolves its conflicts and become socially attached to each other. This is where innovation happens.

Performing is the stage where the team enters the high performance phase.

Adjourning is the stage where the team is disbanded.

Many work groups never get beyond the Storming stage and hence become dysfunctional, never able to achieve the desired wins. Diverse teams are more likely to push through the storming phase, constantly reexamining objective facts.

By breaking up workplace homogeneity, employees become more aware of their own potential biases — entrenched ways of thinking that can otherwise blind them to key information and even lead them to make errors in decision-making processes. According to the report **Cultural Diversity, Innovation, and Entrepreneurship:**

Firm-level Evidence from London, teams with diverse management are more likely to introduce new product innovations than are those with homogeneous "top teams" particularly for reaching international markets. When companies begin to employ 'BLIND' growth strategies they will 'SEE' an Invisible Talent Market where **"Diversity is an economic asset with a social benefit."**

III.   **CREATE APPRENTICESHIPS**

The U.S. Social Class Ladder

Social Class	Education	Occupation	Income	Percentage of Population
Capitalist	Prestige university	Investors and heirs, a few executives	$500,000+	1%
Upper Middle	College or university, often with postgraduate study	Professionals and upper managers	$90,000+	14%
Lower Middle	At least high school; perhaps some college or apprenticeship	Semiprofessionals and lower managers, craftspeople, foremen	About $40,000	30%
Working Class	High school	Factory workers, clerical workers, retail sales, low-paid craftspeople	About $30,000	30%
Working Poor	Some high school	Laborers, service workers, low-paid salespeople	About $18,000	22%
Underclass	Some high school	Unemployed and part-time, on welfare	About $10,000	3%

Source: Based on Gilbert, Dennis, and Joseph A. Kahl. *The American Class Structure: A New Synthesis*. 4th ed. Homewood, Ill.: Dorsey Press, 1993. Income estimates follow Duff, Christina. "Profiling the Aged: Fat Cats or Hungry Victims?" *Wall Street Journal*, September 28, 1995a: B1, B8.

America is known around the world as the land of opportunity, the place where a person can move from the bottom of the social class ladder from underclass to capitalist. The social class ladder is defined by education, career and income rather than a permanent caste system. Ideally, the higher levels of educational attainment and skills a person possesses, the higher they could climb this social ladder.

It is more difficult for Blacks living below middle class to acquire the skills to move up the ladder. When this group matriculates to post-secondary training, the financial aid intended to assist them does not provide the room and board refund until the 9th week of a 12 week semester. How does one live without money for 9 weeks? Many opt to work full time and attend school part-time elongating the degree acquisition process from 2 years for an Associates to 5 years and 4 years for a Bachelors to 7 years. Many eventually dropout as the need for basic necessities over the long-term becomes so great and overwhelming to balance a full time job, part-time school and children.

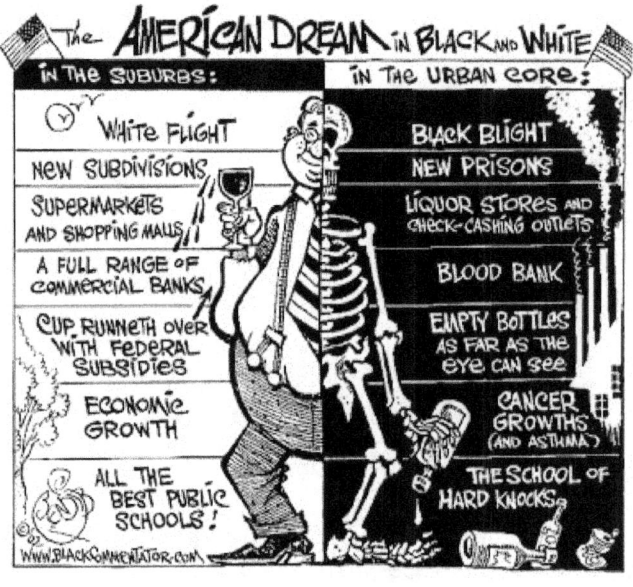

The American Dream for Blacks on the lower rungs of the social ladder, collectively, is a nightmare. Pew Charitable Trust noted 62% of Americans raised in the top fifth income remain in the top two-fifths and conversely 65% raised in the bottom fifth remain in the bottom two-fifths. "Family background plays a more important role in the US," states Corak an economist at University of Ottawa. Americans enjoy less economic mobility than their peers in Canada and much of Western Europe. Even Representative Paul D. Ryan, a Wisconsin Republican who argues that overall mobility remains high, recently wrote that "mobility from the very bottom up" is "where the United States lags behind." A Family Affair: Intergenerational Social Mobility across the Organization for Economic Co-Operation and Development (OECD) Countries finds that social mobility between generations is dramatically lower in the U.S. than in many other developed countries.

According to the OECD report, the main cause of social immobility is educational opportunity. The report states, "It turns out that America's public school system, rather than lifting children up, is instead holding them down."

Secondary schools were intended to prepare individuals for postsecondary training and work. Black secondary schools have done a poor job of preparing students for iSTEAM work and post-secondary training as many do not offer computer science or programming classes.

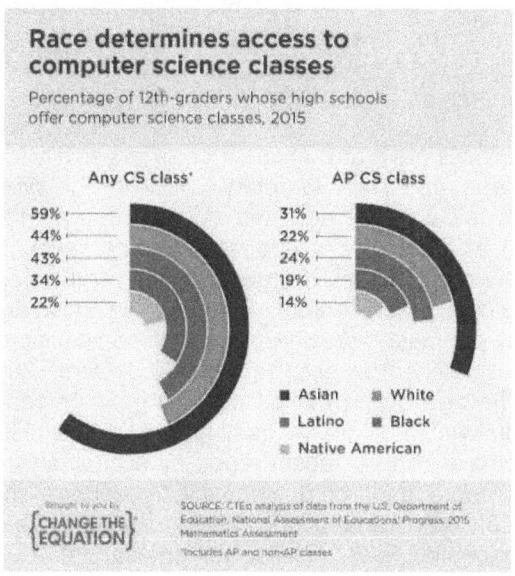

Many students are interested in iSTEAM careers, but spend extra time to complete postsecondary training in these specialties as they have to relearn the subject matter. Blacks are pursuing liberal arts degrees to quickly secure a credential for upward mobility, only to learn any Associates or Bachelor's degree does not guarantee movement into the middle class.

Apprenticeships, internships, co-ops or Learn N Earn programs can solve this dilemma as they are training with a wage. "Today in America, fewer than 5 percent of young people train as apprentices, the overwhelming majority in the construction trades. In Germany, the number is closer to 60 percent—in fields as diverse as advanced manufacturing, IT, banking, and hospitality." In Europe, apprenticeships are called "dual training" as trainees split their days between classroom instruction at a vocational school and on-the-job time at a company. The theory they learn in class is reinforced by the practice at work. Apprentices also learn work habits, skills and responsibility. The bonus trainees are paid for their time, including in class. The apprenticeship arrangement lasts for two to four years, depending on the sector. Both employer and employee generally hope it will lead to a permanent job.

Apprentices are a crucial talent pool," especially for those over age 40. The Secretary of State for Work and Pensions Damian Green said: "Most people are healthier for longer and so are able to extend their careers and take up new opportunities. I urge all businesses to reassess the value of older workers." Figures show those aged 45-59, are the fastest-growing age group participating in UK, approximately, from 9,810 to 41,850 between 2009 and 14. The age group makes up nearly 10 percent of all apprentices who receive training from a business while doing paid work. A recent report by accountants KPMG found 'more and more companies recognize the high value of older workers' knowledge and skills'. There is a misconception older Black workers cannot learn new

Manufacturing Apprenticeships Barely Budge

Industry	FY13 Active Apprentices	FY14 Active Apprentice
Manufacturing	11,129	11,447

Top 25 Active Manufacturing Apprentices FY 2014

Occupation	Active Apprentices
Machinist	1,066
Electrician, Maintenance	1,052
Maintenance Mechanic	1,016
Tool and Die Maker	916
Sheet Metal Worker	654
Chemical Operator III	586
Elevator Constructor Mechanic	532
Refinery Operator	488
Education and Training	406
Machine Operator I	342
Machinist, Outside (Ship)	329
Maintenance Repairer, Industrial	302
Machine Repairer, Maintenance	291
Electrician (Ship & Boat)	280
Electrician	277
Welder, Combination	252
Millwright	243
Line Maintainer	199
Pipe Fitter (Const)	195
Electromechanical Tech	195
Shipfitter (Ship & Boat)	179
Structural Steel/Ironworker	176
Pipe Fitter (Ship & Boat)	174
Mold Maker, Die-Cast & Plastic	162
Production Technologist	158

technology. Gen Xers were the first generation to embrace personal computers, video game consoles and cell phones. They are still active video game players, hence they are trainable in technology as they are immersed in technology every single day.

Many American companies are interested in apprenticeships, except they are not investing in this training. There are an estimated 2 million unfilled skilled trade jobs in construction, healthcare, information technology, manufacturing, yet there were only 410,000 apprentices enrolled with 11,447 in a manufacturing company. Manufacturers, must invest in solving the talent shortage with apprenticeships.

Manufacturers are bemoaning the potential cost. Yes, the short term cost and compliance may appear high and cumbersome if a corporation goes it alone. If they partner with a nonprofit, the cost and compliance can be significantly reduced by Federal grants, foundational grants and personal financial aid. The Federal Government treats co-op as full time college enrollment. This means Apprentices could receive a refund for living expenses while working and the corporation could reduce the working wage to make the apprenticeship more affordable. Secondary schooling should include a 2 year apprenticeship for every student to acquire applicable digital skills and at least 1 workforce credential.

IV. REPLACE BLACK SECONDARY SCHOOLS WITH INVENTION CENTERS

During the Agricultural and Industrial Revolutions, Blacks proliferated in skilled trades learning by doing and then invented new or improved products and services. Blacks invented and secured 365 patents from 1866 to 1950 with the assistance of Historical Black Colleges and Universities (HBCUs).

The Land-Grant College Act of 1862, known as the Morrill Act created colleges that provided an applied science curriculum to power the growth of the Industrial Revolution amongst the working class. Cornell, Massachusetts Institute of Technology (MIT) and Michigan State University (MSU) are some of the more famous land grant colleges. MSU was the first Land grant college. Historical Black Colleges and Universities in 1890 were created in the second wave of Morrill Act providing institutions land and funding from the Federal government as the many of the original land grant colleges refused to admit Blacks. Here are the 16 institutions are:

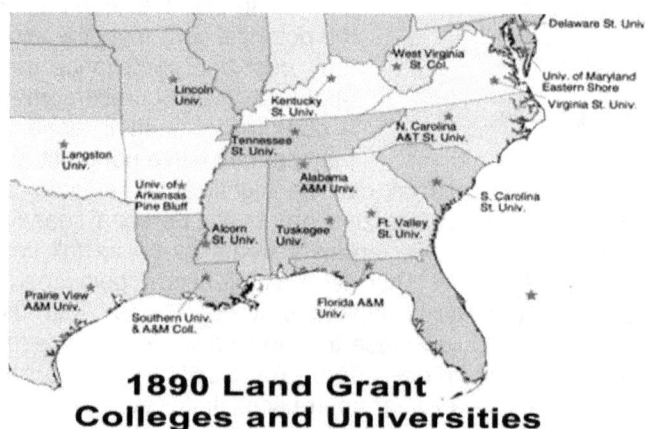

1890 Land Grant Colleges and Universities

Source: USDA. Cooperative State Research Education and Extension

Traditional universities taught classical liberal arts curriculum. The 1890 Land Grant Colleges law, intended to reduce the dearth of skills after slavery, provided for skilled instruction in these applied (hands-on) science areas, as Booker T. Washington referred to as an industrial education:

Agriculture: horticulture, forestry, agronomy, animal husbandry, dairying, veterinary medicine, poultry husbandry, and agriculture

Mechanic arts: Engineering specialties - mechanical, civil, electrical, irrigation, mining, marine, railway, experimental, textile industry, architecture, machine design, mechanical drawing, ceramics, stenography, typewriting, telegraphy, printing, and shop work

Mathematical sciences: mathematics, bookkeeping, and astronomy

Natural and physical sciences: chemistry, physics, biology, botany, zoology, geology, mineralogy, metallurgy, entomology, physiology, bacteriology, pharmacy, physical geography, and meteorology

Economic sciences: political economy, home economics, commercial geography, and sociology

HBCUs expanded career options for Blacks during the Industrial Revolution:

- 80 percent of all Blacks who received MD and DDS were trained at--Howard University and Meharry Medical College.
- 75% of all Blacks holding a doctorate degree;
- 80% of all Black federal judges.
- 37% of Bachelor's degrees to Blacks in the life sciences, physical sciences, mathematics, and engineering.
- 20% of all Blacks holding a Bachelor's degree

According to the Brookings Institute, HBCUs are doing a better job than the average postsecondary institution in social mobility, in terms of vaulting lowest-income young people into the top quintile as adults. HBCUs understand and know the struggles Black students face. They are able to remediate their skills with dignity, pride of culture and vision for the future. They provide a nurturing environment for Black students to make the transition to becoming cultured and educated.

HBCUs were a new vehicle added to accelerate the training of the Black working class during the Industrial

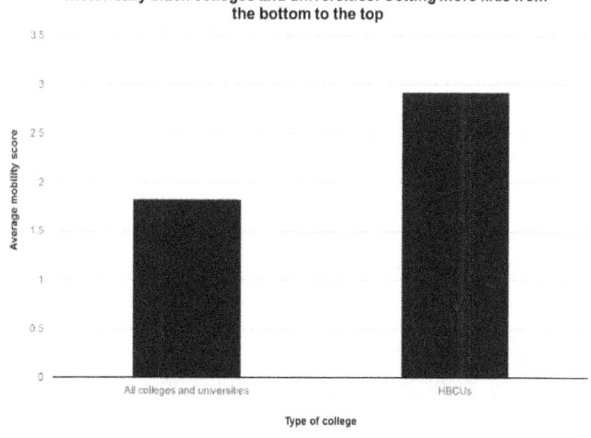

Historically black colleges and universities: Getting more kids from the bottom to the top

Source: Raj Chetty, John N. Friedman, Emmanuel Saez, Nicholas Turner, and Danny Yagan. Online Table 1, Mobility Report Cards: The Role of Colleges in Intergenerational Mobility. The Equal Opportunity Project.

BROOKINGS

Revolution with an applied science curriculum. Invention centers should be the new vehicle for training secondary students for the digital revolution.

Invention - the Economic Engine

From 1940-2000, America experienced an average growth rate of **26.6%**. The growth rate 2000-2009 was **0%**. In 2016, urban communities, like Detroit, were the most severely affected as unemployment is eclipsing 24.8% and underemployment over 50%. The growth rate was negative. Economic developers desire to grow their economies. Corporations desire to grow their profits. In the article, **Invention Is the Mother of Economic Growth: Nathan Myhrvold** former Chief Technology Officer at Microsoft and co-founder of Intellectual Ventures states, *"there is a magical engine for economic growth. It is invention -- the process by which the human mind creates new ideas with practical consequences. Invention and its weaker cousin, innovation, are ultimately the source of all wealth and luxuries."* Entire new companies are evolved or introduced. Inventions can create value in the marketplace or create entirely new marketplaces.

Invention is the art of creation. It is the ultimate source of all that's new. Intellectual Property - every gizmo, gadget, technique or tool - is invented on this exciting journey where the minds' creativity is harnessed and applied to produce a novel solution to a problem. The history of the world is, to a large extent, the history of invention. Some inventions are small incremental improvements while others are radical and transformative breakthroughs. Invention, which is the most important and most difficult part of technology creation, is systematically given the least attention.

Albert Einstein states, "Imagination is more important than knowledge. Imagination leads to creativity, the process of making order out of the seemingly random. Unfortunately, the practice of invention is rarely taught in schools, perhaps because it requires independent thinking and exploration. School systems throughout the world teach theoretical rationale problem solving punishing play, imagination and daydreaming. Invention begins with examining and reframing a problem to see the hidden obvious - the detail and specificity to create a clear picture of what needs to be solved.

Most inventions involve taking something that is already known and making it new in some way, changing the design and/ or functionality. Artistic Design is the embodiment of invention that requires creativity to make elegance - doing the most with the least. Functionality comes from the algorithms or series of steps used repeatedly to make the invention work. Algorithms are the necessary math of inventions, whether the invention is a fancy shampoo bottle, mobile app or service. Residents need an environment where math, imagination, failure and prototyping can flourish. Prototyping is seen as a way to show an idea but it is a way to stimulate mental development of the idea. True economic growth begins with invention and prototyping. I always state, "True economic growth begins with an idea in one's hands."

Invention Centers - "A New Wine in a New Bottle"

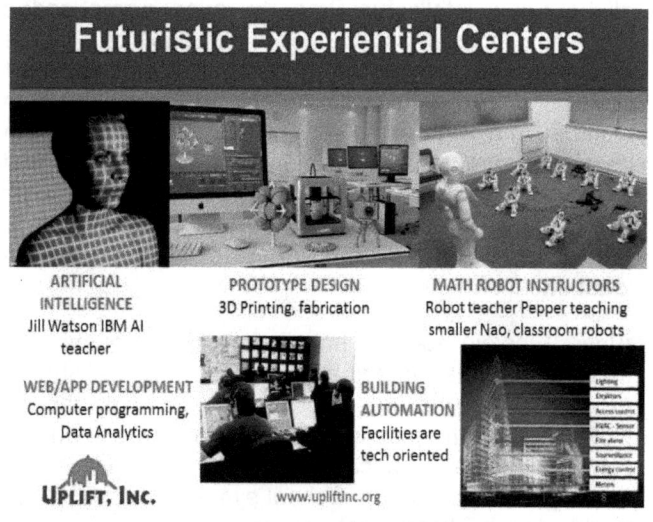

Imagine a shiny high tech futuristic center full of robot instructors, artificial intelligence bots, prototype design, invention classes, community sourced invention competitions, web development classes, IT& Data Analytics Apprenticeships, Building automation, Radically Creative Hands-On invention, Science, Technology, Engineering, Arts and Mathematics (iSTEAM) exhibits to stimulate tech discussions and community invention with corporate America.

Imagine this invention center sitting in a blighted Detroit neighborhood where residents are exposed to future technology before the general consumer market. A center where residents, both students ages 12-18 and their parents, receive hands-on skills-based training, prototype design instruction and support along with the soft skills of liberal arts delivered via technology. Would this high-tech futuristic invention center incubate a creative invention vibe? Would it motivate residents to acquire skills to complete their invention and perhaps skills to obtain a high demand job, too? Would this high-tech futuristic invention center push commercialization of inventions?

Would Corporate America coalesce in this center to perform live market research in the product/ service invention process? Would the growth of start-ups accelerate? Would Corporate America create new jobs due to speed up the invention process? Would Corporate America partner and contract with these new start-ups?

TECH INTERSECTION FORUM
Future Tech discussions

HANDS-ON iSTEAM EXHIBITS

ESPORTS & VIDEO GAME TOURNAMENTS

IT & DATA ANALYST APPRENTICESHIPS

UPLIFT, INC.

HUB FOR NEIGHBORHOOD INTERNET SERVICE

www.upliftinc.org

INVISIBLE TALENT MARKET 101

Would this high-tech futuristic invention center increase income levels and reduce poverty? Would hopelessness, crime and blight be forced out of communities?

Johann Wolfgang von Goethe quotes, "Treat people as if they were what they ought to be and you help them to become what they are capable of being." Currently, working class and underclass people across America are treated as the scum of the earth. Almost everything in their world screams PERMANENT FAILURE, which is why failure is so prevalent in their neighborhoods. Incubate the future in the Black community and the entire economy of inner cities will rev upward.

"Same Old Wine in New Bottles
Few Black students are properly prepared with rigorous engaging courses to sail easily through post-secondary training. Approximately 59.3% of Blacks drop out of four-year institutions compared to 39.3% of Whites. Secondary schools in Black communities are the bottleneck in the talent pipeline, causing a severe talent shortage.

When Blacks began to attend secondary schools in the 1950s run by Whites, they lost their ability to invent and secure patents. Teachers forced mere book education stripping away the "industrial education that provided the skills that makes labor valuable. Blacks no longer "played" with skills or the trades. Schools suppressed Blacks "kinesthetic learning style". Blacks are students who have to do, who have to be active, who have to have hands-on. Most urban classrooms aren't set up to adapt to that learning style. White suburban schools accelerated their introduction of this kinesthetic curriculum as it better prepared students for post-secondary training.

Yet, the discussion of urban education continually evolves around governance structures – traditional public, charters or private, rather than the retooling of the curriculum/ pedagogy that has never worked for Blacks. Governed by Bloom's Taxonomy since 1956, Public schools provide school curriculum should be taught in a cumulative ladders of levels. The average Black school spends inordinate time teaching at levels 1-2 (Remembering and Understanding) of Bloom's Taxonomy whereas middle/ high school standardized exams test at level 6 (Creating). Experimentation, inventing and problem solving are the ultimate goal of education.

Bloom's Taxonomy

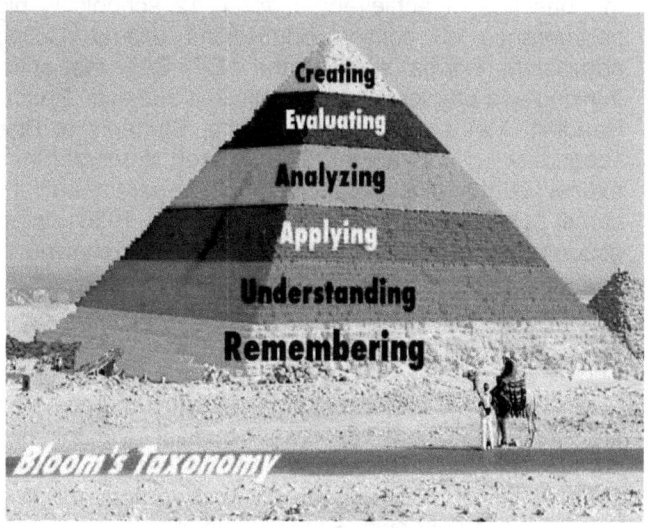

Level 1   Remembering   Recall knowledge from long-term memory.

Level 2   Understanding Construct meaning from oral, written, and graphic messages

Level 3   Applying   Execute or implement a procedure

Level 4   Analyzing   Determine how the parts relate to one another and to an overall structure

Level 5   Evaluating   Use criteria for judgments

Level 6   Creating   Reorganize elements into a new pattern or structure

Standardized exams test seek to see who has the ability to invent and create intellectual property to solve problems. Since most corporations operate on the belief invention formally called research and development (R&D) happens with individuals with the most degrees, the baseline of achievement for K-12 schools is high performance on college admissions exams. College admissions exams, such as the ACT/ SAT, test critical thinking and problem solving skills in 4 subjects: English, Reading, Mathematics and Science. Students at Black secondary schools are hardly prepared to master these exams as their instruction did not prepare them. The same substandard school conditions in 1930s is still occurring in the 2000s. Blacks have never received the funding or highly qualified teachers necessary for the masses to be successful on any college admissions exam or intelligence test.

Cathy Duffy in *Government Nannies*, documented urban schools provide diluted curriculum that stifles imagination, critical thinking, innovation and invention. Hence, students within these schools are unprepared for college by no fault of their own. For example, classes in schools that serve the middle class or upper-middle class population would include residential architecture, the designing of commercial structures, broadcast journalism, advanced computer graphics, a sophisticated course in furniture design, carving and sculpture, 3D-Animation or an honors course in engineering research and design. At many Black schools, in contrast, these courses are basic without hands-on experimentation. Difficult subjects like STEM - Science, Technology, Engineering and Mathematics - are often taught straight from a textbook rather than in a laboratory format that forces innovation, critical thinking or problem solving skills. Even when a course title denotes college preparatory, its students often receive a diluted course.

I experienced this first hand as my twins in 2009 were exposed to this curriculum dilution in a Detroit application magnet high school. Here is an email exchange regarding a physics class which incidentally is scheduled for seniors, fully knowing juniors are tested in Physics on the ACT, the required state exam under No Child Left Behind.

Here is the excerpt of emails I wrote to Detroit Public Schools regarding the absence of labs in an 11th grade AP (Advanced Placement) Physics class. This saga went on for 9 weeks into the 12 week Physics semester: *(Names replaced with XXXX to protect the guilty.)*

Email #1 to Principal   10/7/2009
While I know you have a lot on your plate, I must begin to drill into my children's curriculum. We have entered another year of science without hands-on experiments.

We cannot afford another lecture-based year. I sent an email to Mr. XXXX regarding those experiments .I did not have Mrs. XXXX email or I would have sent her the same. I will be visiting on Tuesday. Please prepare the pacing guides and the experiment list for both Physics classes. I also want a list of the hands-on labs associated with Algebra 3. Please have those available as well. Are there field trips for any of their classes?

Email # 9   10/22/2009
I received the supplementary Problems Physics Home Lab the Graphical Analysis of Motion.

1. The basis of what scientists believe is the result of the careful collection and analysis of laboratory evidence. In any physics class, the differentness of science will be most evident when it comes time for lab. In physics class**, lab is central.** Integral. Sacred. More than a mere place in the back of the classroom, the laboratory is the place where physics students **do** physics. It is in the laboratory that physics students learn to practice the activities of scientists - asking questions, performing procedures, collecting data, analyzing data, answering questions, and thinking of new questions to explore.

2. This assignment is not a physics experiment held within a laboratory at XXX it is an assignment sent home to appease me. Well I am not appeased.

3. Neither Mr. XXXX nor XXXX have conducted 2 labs without required lab reports for the labs they did perform. Every High School in Michigan is required to teach the scientific inquiry process as defined by the Michigan High School Content Expectation (HSCE) created 10/06. Your teachers have not taught the formal scientific inquiry process as that process is based in lab experiments. Whatever was taught prior to 10/06 it is to be scrapped as recreated based on these 10/06 HSCEs.

4. Given the fact you have only had 1 **real** physics lab conducted by the teacher, it is inappropriate for the students to be expected to setup a lab at home when they have hardly seen their professionally trained physics teacher conduct a lab at school within a laboratory stocked with equipment.

5. Again for the 5th time, I am requesting a schedule of Physics experiments. Here is XXXX's Physics schedule (Click on link). If XXXX can establish a schedule so can XXXX.

6. Since it appears we are not connecting in what a physics experiment is, I have found several at experiments (Click on link) for my children's class that relates to the subject they are studying. **(This is the website for High School Physics class where they have 56 labs a year. If they can do it, so can XXX)**. Here are more experiments. Please complete a lab (not a mathematical problem) next week. Since I will be out of town, Please film the lab and email me both the video and each student's typewritten completed lab report.

7. It is quite obvious the teachers are refusing to compile with my basic request. I am expecting that you have completed a discipline write up for both Mr. XXXX and Ms. XXXX for failure to complete Physics Labs. Every week Mr. XXXX and Ms. XXXX does not perform a lab, I am expecting another write-up until they are both dismissed from XXXX.

I received a list of experiments 11/9/2009 9 weeks into a 12 week class and students had a second experiment during the same week compared to their affluent counterparts who had 14 experiments during the same time period. The experiments they did have looked like replications of experiments they had during middle school. The experiments did not require students to problem solve, innovate or invent. Can you believed Grosse Pointe South (an extremely wealthy suburb) Advanced Placement Physics class has 56 labs annually while a Detroit Public School's Detroit School of Arts Advanced Placement Physics Class had 5 labs over the same time period? It is any wonder why young struggle to score high on college admissions exams or complete postsecondary credentials. They are missing the basics in high school STEM classes with the most fundamental class being - mathematics.

My twins matriculated to college with scholarships. Karen matriculated to Western Michigan University (WMU) to pursue a Bachelors in Business administration and Kevin matriculated to Rochester Institute of Technology (RIT) to pursue a Bachelors in Information Technology. Both struggled through their math and science classes. While they had Advance Placement courses in high school, they were not nearly as rigorous as college courses as they were severely missing the lab assignments. They survived their courses as they had the support of college educated parents who battled with a school system to get some elements they needed. Blacks need a different curriculum. They need "A New Wine in a New Bottle"

"Invention in Action".
In 2004, my, then, 10 year genius son asked me why he needed to sit for 7 hours a day listening to his teachers lecture him when he could read the material in 2 hours on the internet thereby saving the next 5 hours to do hands-on projects. While researching project-based learning, invention and tech, I stumbled upon an economic report by Professor Jeff Brice, Jr. *Legitimate and Illicit Entrepreneurship: An Opinion Concerning the Relation of Convergent and Divergent Business Development Strategies*, where he stated "Organized crime is a functional part of the American social system that, primarily, minorities and immigrants have used as a means of upward mobility." African American and Puerto Rican crime organizations follow the entrepreneurial network, the same model as the small businessperson. He stated, "**A drug dealer is really an entrepreneur who is simply selling the wrong products.**" They are selling illegal products as someone provided the product or showed them how to create the product. Nonetheless

their secondary schools never taught them how to invent. His economics research was confirmed by 50 years of elite researchers at Harvard, Yale, Stanford, University of California, University of Michigan and others who drug dealers share the same traits with entrepreneurs operating on the right side of the law: Both are risk-takers, each collaborates with others, they aspire to wealth, and demonstrate competence in their chosen fields, which each demand intelligence, dependability, and self-confidence. Professors McCarthy of UC Davis and John Hagan of Northwestern University showed in their 2001 study, *When Crime Pays: Capital, Competence, and Criminal Success*, that drug dealers generated higher incomes, nearly three times, than those employed in traditional jobs available for young people. The Zip Code where a student lives and their families' economic status determines where they land in adulthood.

Not Intelligence.   Not Ideas.   Not Work Ethic.

White Affluent students with entrepreneurial traits are groomed with hands-on invention lessons from kindergarten through high school graduation. They are then provided with financial support to turn their invention research during k-12 into a startup venture by ages 18-22.

Black poverty stricken students with the same entrepreneurial traits are **CRUSHED** with theoretical factual non-invention oriented lessons. Many students receive less than 3 hours of science instruction weekly beginning in the 4th grade, causing mass failure on standardized science exams, like NAEP, for the next 8 years.

They are never able to catch up with their White suburban colleagues. Students become ridiculed, humiliated and stereotyped as failures until they become behavior/discipline problems. These students are then labeled behavioral and emotionally impaired. They normally land in the school graveyard - **SPECIAL EDUCATION.** Sixty-nine (69%) percent of Detroit students in Special education do not graduate from high school Leaving them no honest alternatives for their future (*Michigan* Consortium for *Education Research, 2011)* Professor McCarthy argues, *"it's simply adverse circumstances -- a tight job market, a lack of education -- that lead young people into crime. We are losing all sorts of valuable resources by not providing sufficient opportunities in the economy for these bright people. We bear a considerable cost imprisoning people like this who could make a contribution in the legal economy."* In his 1989 Presidential Address to the National Economic Association, Professor Samuel Myers, Jr., criticized policy makers for not exploiting *"the entrepreneurial talents of street-wise hustlers and dope-dealers in the inner city to enable them to become managers and owners of legitimate inner city businesses."*

Armed with this economic research, my nonprofit set out to test the theory of invention as an economic driver by building an alternative high school, Hustle & TECHknow Preparatory High School for high school dropouts and adjudicated youth in a 1.5 billion dollar software developer. In 2006, we won a contract with the local school district to construct a futuristic school with a cyber and invention based curriculum.

We discovered school curriculum and the environment of its implementation has been the same for almost 100 years. By changing the curriculum and instituting a futuristic high tech environment, we changed the results.

Hustle & TECHknow Preparatory High School was shut down to make way for the charter school expansion, which 10 years later in Detroit, has not produced a mass quantity of thinkers, innovators and inventors, corporations desire. In the same time frame, we completed more invention–oriented projects to garner these results:

Community Workshops
- Automation Workz - Prepared 2782 people, Parents & Students with hands-on Math/ Invention skills 2013-2017
- Escape to College -Assisted 30 adults matriculate to college in 2010 and 50 in 2011 100 in 2012

Developed Prototype
- Developed Fluke –the wealth building game of accidental inventions. Sold 150 copies.
- Performed 110 parent workshops

Harper Woods Middle/ High School
- Invention Adventure Summer Camp at Harper Woods High 2012 & 2013 for 30 students

John R. King Performing Arts
- Increased MEAP Math proficiency scores 2013 by 225% and 2012 by 300%.
- Increased MEAP Science proficiency scores 2013 by 181%.

Detroit School of Arts
- Increased 2008 MME Math proficiency scores 38.43%,
- Increased 2008 MME Science by 15.89%

Hustle & TECHknow Preparatory High School
- Compiled Reading class that moved student collective Lexile reading grades 3.6 from 4.2 to 7.8
- Recruited 600 students for 130 slots at contract school
- Sent three quarterfinalists out of 79 to the National Vocabulary Championship
- 80% graduation rate, 100% postsecondary matriculation
- Attendance Rate increased to 96%, Increased Parent Participation Rate to 70%
- Increased Collective Grade Point Average 1.612 points (from .738 to 2.35)

- Won Educational Program of the Year 2007, Automation Alley; First Wayne County school to win

Can you believe these students were high school dropouts and adjudicated youth?

Duke Ellington Conservatory of Music and Art
- Increased MEAP Middle School Reading proficiency scores 2005 by 90.9%
- Increased MEAP Middle School Math MEAP proficiency scores 2006 by 331.25%

Hanstein Elementary
- Increased 2003 MEAP Math proficiency scores 76.72%, 2003 MEAP Reading by 177.94%

Invention and Play
Dr. Stuart Brown, Author, **Play** and Professor, Stanford D. School quotes,

Nations (states, cities, neighborhoods, corporations) ***that remain economically strong are those that can create intellectual property – and the ability to innovate largely comes out of an ability to play,"***

Evan Schwartz, in his book, **Juice**, highlighted that flashes of genius world renowned inventors, such as Woody Norris, Steve Jobs, and Bill Gates exhibited are derived from their childlike proclivity to play with the things that interest them. This connection of invention and play has been documented in research and many books. Plato in 427 BC stated, "*A man must practice that thing from early childhood, in play as well as earnest, with all the attendant circumstances of the action. We should seek to use games as a means of directing children's tastes and inclinations toward the station they are themselves to fill when adult.*" "Play and imitation are natural learning strategies. Having individuals play games to learn is simply asking them to do what comes naturally." "Play provides individuals, both students and family leaders, the ability to explore and experiment on their own terms."

Play turns a mundane task into fun as play is soulful, pleasurable and exhilarating. When people are having fun, they forget it is work, meaning they stay on task a lot longer extending the learning process. Play allows individuals to model the learning process and professions naturally. Modeling prepares students for the challenging work—for framing problems; finding, integrating and

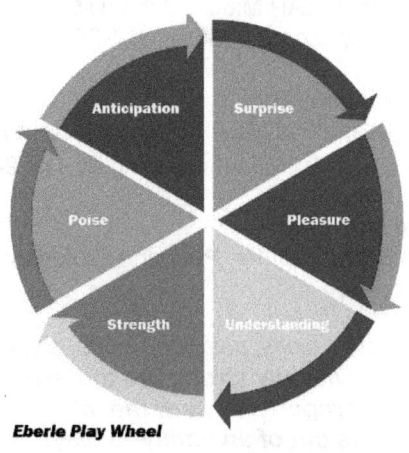

Eberle Play Wheel

synthesizing information; creating new solutions; learning on their own; and working cooperatively. Play leads to innovation or profitable invention. The irony, Play has been squeezed out of school, and the community. Play has been criminalized as a behavior issue. The focus of schools and workforce development should be play.

Eberle Play Wheel was created in 2009 by Dr. Scott Eberle VP of Play Studies at Strong Museum of Play, summarizes the play process. Eberle Play Wheel begins with Curiosity, a form of anticipation, the first element, leads to surprise and discovery, the second. Pleasure, the third element, functions as an incentive to play some more. Pleasure leads to understanding, the fourth element, providing capacity for insight. The fifth element, strength—flows from understanding.

Play trains our physical skills, sharpens our mental abilities, and deepens our insights into our social capabilities. Players garner strength in the form of mastery and control. When we play on words, solve puzzles, choose sides, or sing silly songs, we enlarge our working vocabularies, practice and stimulate our sense of numbers and proportions, train our wit, maintain our friendships, augment our sense of fairness, and exercise our feeling for rhythm.

Much of the pleasure from play is social in nature, and play strengthens social skills. Playing also deliberately rearranges relationships and enhances social wit. At play we learn to read others' intentions to deflect and defuse conflict. Play contributes to our composure and ease. This composure, in turn, spreads Wit, ingenuity, creativity, drive, and passion, all expressions of strength and poise, the sixth and final element of play. Play is the foundation of invention.

Eberle Play Wheel is quite similar to the Bloom's Taxonomy. Both are processes for learning with six parts, except Play allows for experiential learning or scientifically modeling through the entire process. The National

Academy of Science in its book, **How People Learn: Brain, Mind, Experience, and School Expanded Edition 2000**, quotes, "It (*Modeling*) is central to professional practice in many disciplines, such as mathematics and science, but it is largely missing from school instruction. Taking a model-based approach to a problem entails inventing (or selecting) a model, exploring the qualities of the model, and then applying the model to answer a question of interest." Play includes application through inventing. The National Academy of Science confirms this Plato's quote in the *Plato, Laws, Bk. 1 643b-643d,* "their tutors with miniature tools on the pattern of real ones. In particular, all necessary preliminary instruction should be acquired in this way. Thus, the carpenter should be taught by his play to use the rule and the plumb line, and the soldier to sit a horse, and the like."

Corporate America is experiencing the greatest talent shortage in the skilled trades. Blacks having served in skilled trades for 250 years. They have the ability to eliminate the talent shortage if secondary schools provided experiential learning as Plato suggests. Experiential learning is any learning that supports students in applying their knowledge and conceptual understanding to real-world problems or situations. It is applied learning, learning by doing, using case and problem-based studies, guided inquiry, simulations, experiments, invention or art projects. Experiential learning is based on this ideology:

Learners grasp...
10% of what they read
20% of what they hear
30% of what they hear with a visual accompaniment
50% of what they experience with a live demo
90% of what they experience for themselves via a simulation

Tech universities, such as Massachusetts Institute of Technology (MIT), Rochester Institute of Technology

(RIT), California Institute of Technology (Cal Tech), and Kettering, have experiential learning curriculums. Thirty years ago, middle and high schools had experiential applied learning classes titled - Blueprinting, Woodworking, Metal shop, Drafting, Home Economics, Mechanics. These classes have been eliminated in urban secondary schools, except for the 11th and 12th graders enrolled in career technical education.

According to Jawanza Kujufu, author of **Understanding Black Learning Styles**, when school districts implemented experiential learning, scores on standardized exams rose from the 30th percentile to the 83rd percentile in North Carolina and from the 30th percentile to the 78th percentile in Louisiana.

Despite the success of invention and experiential learning, urban secondary schools and workforce development programs refuse to embrace invention and experiential learning to prepare students for the world of work and post-secondary training. It is time to invent a new educational vehicle to solve the digital revolution talent shortage. It is time to implement **INVENTION CENTERS**.

Invention centers have the potential to incubate a profitable future in the middle of a blighted inner city. They have the potential to make up lost economic and social progress eradicating poverty, crime, low post-secondary matriculation and entrepreneurship.

Inner cities, like Detroit, need invention centers so Corporate America can '**SEE**' the Invisible Talent Market available to expand economic profitability during this Digital Revolution, just as Blacks did during the Agricultural Revolution, Industrial Revolution and the multiplicity of Wars.

The only 3 questions that remain:

1. Will your leadership continue to embrace the bias that perpetuates the myth there is no diverse talent in the immediate pipeline?

2. Is your corporate leadership committed to training Blacks to expand your profits?

3. Will you erect artificial barriers to social mobility then ask why Blacks are not qualified for future jobs?

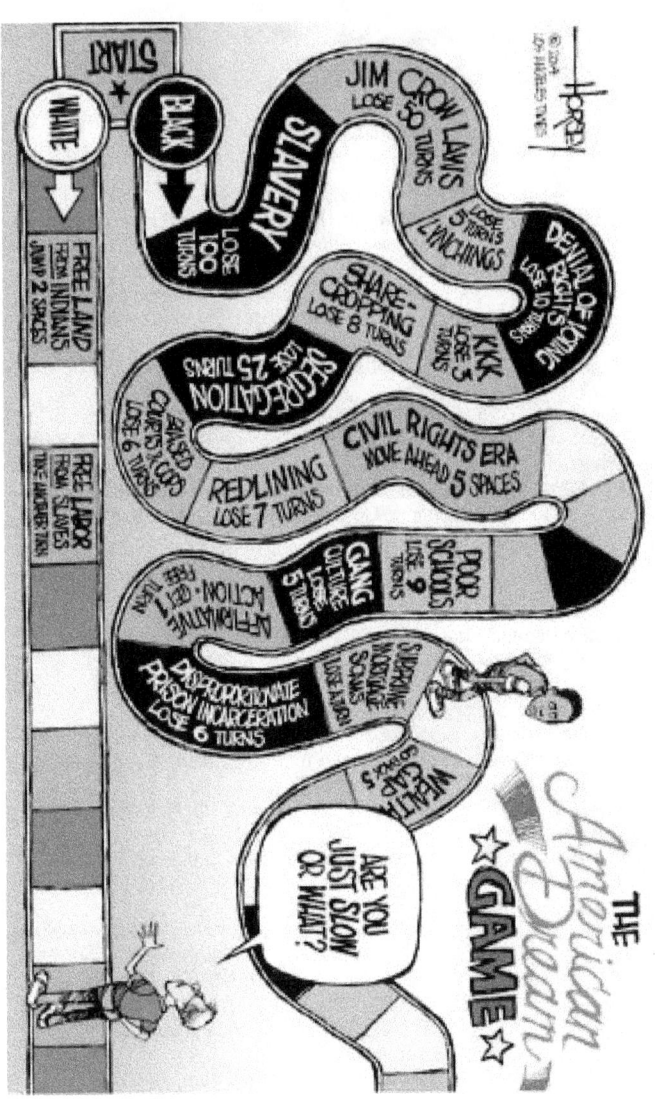

INVISIBLE TALENT MARKET   117

Reference

Here are cited research sources that have not been written directly into book text.

Chapter 1   Change in the Air Under President Trump Regime
New York Post. *I will be the greatest jobs president that God has ever created: Trump*, 5/16/15 Reuters
Baur, C. and Wee, D. *Manufacturing's Next Act*, McKinsey & Co. 2015
Rutkin, A. *Report Suggests Nearly Half of US Jobs are Vulnerable to Computerization*, MIT Technology Review, 9/12/13
Webster, MJ. *Where the Jobs Are: The New Blue Collar*, USA Today 9/3/14
Auerbach, D. *18 High-Paying Non-Desk Jobs*, Career Builder, 4/16/15
Muro, M. *Manufacturing Jobs Aren't Coming Back*, MIT Technology Review, 11/18/16
PISA 2015 Results (Volume I) Excellence and Equity in Education, Organization for Economic Co-Operation and Development (OECD) 12/2016

Chapter 2   Blacks Rescued Agricultural Revolution Talent Shortage
MacPherson, J. *Battle Cry of Freedom*, Oxford University Press, 1988
Slavery in America - Black History - HISTORY.com
Pruitt, Sarah. *5 Things You May Not Know About Lincoln, Slavery and Emancipation*, History Channel, 2012
Our Documents. *Transcript of Emancipation Proclamation*
The Mechanics' magazine, museum, register, journal, and gazette. M. Salmon. 1836. pp. 320–. Retrieved 2011
Potter, Joan. *African American Firsts* (New York: Kensington Publishing Group, 2010
Abraham Lincoln: Campaigns and Elections, University of Virginia Miller Center

Chapter 3   Blacks Rescued Industrial Revolution Talent Shortage
Butchart, R. *Freedmen's Education during Reconstruction*, 2002
"Act Passed by the General Assembly of the State of North Carolina at the Session of 1830—1831" (Raleigh: 1831).
The Henry *Baker Papers. List* Of Known African-American Inventors 1845-1980 wbcp1580.com/blkinvlist.pdf
Black History Month - African American Inventors, ThoughtCo

Chapter 4   The Great Migration and Race Riots
Dubois, W.E.B., *The Souls of Black Folks*, Catawba Publishing, 2007
Gibson, Robert A. *The Negro Holocaust: Lynching and Race Riots in the United States,1880-1950*, Yale-New Haven Teachers Institute, 2/1979

Williams, Chad. *Africana Age Americans and World War I*, New York Public Library.
1943 - A race riot there will be http://www.detroits-great-rebellion.com/Detroit---1943.html
Kinder, Carolyn. *Changing Attitudes in America*, Yale-New Haven Teachers Institute, 4/4/1994
PBS. *The War, At Home Civil Rights*
Detroit Race Riot (1967), Black Past,
Detroit's Great Rebellion
Baime, AJ, *The Arsenal of Democracy: FDR, Detroit, and an Epic Quest to Arm an America at War*, 2014
Francis, D. *How 1960's Riots Hurt African Americans*
Collins, W. and Margo, R. *The Labor Market Effects of the 1960s Riots* (National Bureau Economics Research Working Paper 10243),
Collins, W. *The Economic Aftermath of the 1960s Riots: Evidence from Property Values* (National Bureau Economics Research Working Paper 10493),

Chapter 5 Black Brawn vs White Brains
Haroun, C. *A Brief History of Silicon Valley, the Region That Revolutionizes How We Do Everything*, Entrepreneur, 12/8/2014
Stanford University. *History* website
Ellis, A. Golz, R.& Mayrhofer, W. *The Education Systems of Germany and Other European Countries of the 19th Century in the View of American and Russian Classics: Horace Mann and Konstantin Ushinsky, International Dialogues on Education*, 1/5/2014
Rose, j. *How to Break Free of Our 19th-Century Factory-Model Education System*, The Atlantic, 5/9/2012
Jim Crow's Schools, American Federation of Teachers, Website
Florida, R. *Rise of the Creative Class*, 2002
Byrd-Hill, I. *Escape to College*, Upheaval Media LLC 2010
O'Shea,K., Simon, D. and Yan,H. *Dylann Roof's racist rants read in court*, CNN 12/14/2016
Hambrick, D. *The SAT is a Good Intelligence Test*, New York Times 12/16/11
The College Board, *About Us* Collegeboard.com
Eberle, S. *The Elements of Play Toward a Philosophy and a Definition of Play*, Journal of Play, 2014

Chapter 6 Blacks Driving Mobile Tech Usage
Uplift, Inc. *Mobile Profile of the Native Detroiter*, Survey of Automation Workz Registrants, 2017
Cohen, Dan. *It's Not Only Rich Teens That Have Smartphones*, The Atlantic, 4/15/2016

Chapter 7 Underserved = Economic Profit
Boschma, J.*Black Consumers Have 'Unprecedented Impact' in 2015* The Atlantic , 2/2/2016
Land-Grant College Act of 1862 Britannica encyclopedia

Associated Press, *Diversity in tech: Lots of attention, little progress*, 1/28/2017.

Marcus, B. *The Lack Of Diversity In Tech Is A Cultural Issue*, Forbes, 8/12/2015

DePARLE, Jason. *Harder for Americans to Rise from Lower Rungs*, New York Times, 1/4/2012

Froomkin, Don. *Social Immobility: Climbing The Economic Ladder Is Harder In The U.S. Than In Most European Countries*, Huffington Post, 3/17/2010

Anthony, K. *Not Cool: 10 Brands & Companies Accused Of Racial Profiling* , Global Grind,

Hunt, V. Layton, D. and Prince, S. *Why diversity matters*, McKinsey & Co., 2015

McGirt, Ellen, *How Racial Bias Is Showing Up in School*, Fortune, 9/28/2016

Gershenson,S. Holt, Papageorge, N. *Who believes in me? The effect of student–teacher demographic match on teacher expectations* Economics of Education Review June 2016 10.1016/j.econedurev.2016.03.002

Ahmed, S. *Racial disparities persist in U.S. schools*, CNN, 6/7/2016

Boudreau, J. *Zappos Killed the Job Posting – Should You?* Harvard Business Review, 1/28/2016

O'Connell, M. *Empire's' Black (Ratings) Power: How Fox's Targeted Marketing Paid Off*, Hollywood Reporter, 1/28/2015

Jacoby, T. *Why Germany Is So Much Better at Training Its Workers*, The Atlantic , 10/6/2014

Myhrvold, N. *Invention Is the Mother of Economic Growth*, Bloomberg, 2011

Paley, S. *The Art of Invention*, Prometheus Books, 2010

Aptara. *Gamification Makes For Better* Corporate Training 1/29/2016

Desire to 'SEE' the Invisible Talent Market Clearer?

Approach Diversity & Inclusion as a business strategy and exploration tour that will improve your profits and corporate growth.

Skip the lecture-based do's and don'ts workshops and conferences. They are not working. Immerse your executives and employees in Black culture with:

1. **Community Play events**
Arrange a scavenger hunt to serve data collection points, recruiting sources and training tools. Check out Automation Workz www.autoworkz.org

2. **Data mining/ marketing research**
Survey Black residents and employees to determine their needs, wants and desires. Chapter 6 is an example.

3. **Employee Brainstorming sessions**
Play, Invent and Simulate to learn how to devise products, corporate culture and skill training to include Blacks. Experience games like Fluke.

**For more information,
Go to:**
www.upliftinc.org

Contact
Ida Byrd-Hill
313-444-4885
invisible@upliftinc.org

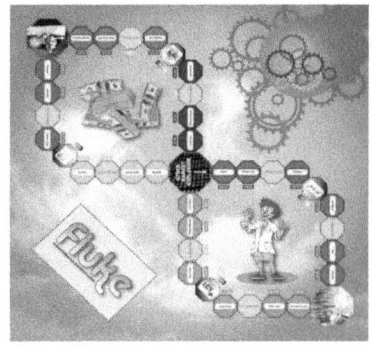

INVISIBLE TALENT MARKET 121

www.ingramcontent.com/pod-product-compliance
Lightning Source LLC
Chambersburg PA
CBHW071729090426
42738CB00011B/2426